STORY ABOUT A MAN
WHO WANTED TO DIE AT HOME

by Martynas Čeledinas

COPYRIGHT

BASED ON A TRUE STORY

"Nobody knows himself truly until he is tested by life."

Author anonymous

My story is different from all the others you might have heard. You may choose to believe it or not. But this is my true story. I grew up in a difficult time. The world was at the brink of war, a horrible war that would haunt us for many years to come. Many people fought in the war and many died for various reasons, my utmost wish is that it should never happen again. The people of my country had a very similar fate to the Russian people who suffered the most from the war. People were sent to death camps, work camps, gulags, and executions were carried out on the Polish, Estonian, Latvian, Ukrainian, Belarusian, Lithuanian and on the Russian people as well. These crimes must be remembered and never forgotten.

You might be wondering why you should listen to me. I'm not a celebrity, I don't have a mansion worth millions of dollars, I don't give performances all over the world, and I didn't go platinum, but I have something many people don't. I have a story to tell. My life story is much more eventful than any story a celebrity could tell; it has something that many people have forgotten. My story is real, it has horror, sacrifice and something that is much more important than gold. It has hope. Hope for a brighter future for those who struggle and are in pain. This is a story that can inspire many people because it wasn't simple and my struggles in life were anything but easy.

Sometimes, I wondered why my life was different from others, why I deserved the fate that was brought upon me. But after some time, I understood that many people in my lifetime and many people all over the world suffered even worse fates.

Humanity has suffered many horrible events in its lifetime. World War II was the most horrible event in history that humanity has faced. The Second World War resulted in 50 million to 85 million fatalities and directly involved more than 100 million people from over 30 countries. This was the second most horrible war that ever happened on a global scale. Eleven million people died during the Holocaust, which wiped out much of the Jewish population in Europe. Many people in small countries were killed, sent to war, imprisoned or left to die of starvation. The food supply was low, so people were fighting over a lump of bread or warm clothes. Every generation should remember that those horrible events that happened in the Second World War should never happen again.

The Russian people suffered the most from the war. The Soviet Union lost an estimated 20,000,000 of its people to war. If any of you think that war is glorious and dying for some righteous cause will be an interesting adventure, you should ask any war veteran you know and he will tell you the real deal. The first casualty of war is the truth and nothing is truer than this. Lies, deception, corruption, terror is commonplace during the time of war. People who start wars are maniacs; they have no regard for human life. War is always a failure of diplomacy and a way for somebody to show off that they are not right in the head.

All wars end the same: horror, hunger, pain, agony, loss of human life, orphans, homeless people, wasted cities, criminals on the loose, lawlessness, no clean water, low food supply, numerous cries at night, shattered lives of men, women, and children.

For your generation, the war had another meaning. Total nuclear war would mean the end of human civilization and every life on planet earth. There is no way to deny it, no way to escape it. This is a great power and an even greater responsibility for the people who are to press the red button and launch nuclear strikes or open some other Pandora's Box.

Now I will tell my story. I had a wonderful childhood. As a child, I used to run through the open fields and when I was tired, I would lie on the grass and look at the sky. The country life wasn't easy. We had to work hard just to survive. Because without work, there was no food on the table. There were no supermarkets back then. I remember, whenever my mother prepared dinner, we would sneak quietly and try to grab a bite while she was preparing dinner. If we were naughty or didn't help her, we would get the "broom treatment." My mother had to be strict because she was responsible for the whole family, and only through discipline and hard work could peasants like us survive. You can survive without Facebook and Google, you can survive without a smartphone and you can even survive without electricity, but you can't survive without food and water. We used to work hard to grow everything by ourselves, day after day. We had no machinery and we worked mostly with just our hands. We planted with our hands, harvested with our hands and did everything mostly on our own. I won't lie, we had a little help. We had horses and they were very valuable because they could do the hard work for us. I had a few brothers and we all went to the lake to relax after all the hard work. It was wonderful. The water was so clean and fresh that we'd never want to leave the shore.

I loved my family. My mom, dad, and brothers were the most important things in my life. I always wanted to be like my father who was the strongest in the family. He was my role model. I wanted to be more like him. My father was a carpenter; he built our house and made furniture for our home. It wasn't something fancy modern like you have today, but it was great at the time we lived in it. He used to make tools for the whole family to work with, like the carriage for the horse, table, and chairs for our home, scythes, sickles and other house items. He didn't make nails or other metal parts, because it was the work of the village blacksmith, but everything else was made by my father, on his own. Back then communities were very important;

our neighbors helped us plant, plow, cut the grass and harvest and we helped them do the same too. We visited the church every Sunday and prayed for a good harvest. My youngest brother wanted to ride the horse, but he couldn't climb onto the animal. He was too little and we always laughed at him, but we helped him out. I would put him on the horse and ride with him through the fields. I knew he liked it and he always smiled holding onto the horse's mane.

Time passed and we grew, little by little. We helped our parents as much as we could. We cut down the grass in vast fields with our hands for our cows and horses and our neighbor's horses, we chopped wood for winter, and we planted and gathered the harvest. We had a wonderful time with good friends from neighboring farms who helped us. We didn't have as much technology as you have today, but our food was healthy, our water was clean and we had everything we needed. I had to go to school, which was located many kilometers away from our home. Back then, there were very few schools and very few educated people, so everybody was trying to learn.

I remember one day, I was returning from school when it was getting dark. I heard a wolf howling. When I saw those shining and sparkling wolf's eyes in the dark, it was the scariest thing I had ever seen before, those glowing eyes in the night gave me chills. The animal was very frightening; it had the teeth of a beast that could rip you in pieces, especially when I was little. Fortunately, my father always escorted me back from school in the nighttime and always kept an ax with him, for wolves. I was scared and wanted to get out of the woods as fast as I could. But wolves are just animals; they act on instinct. The scariest animals in this world are people. There are some people you should be really scared of. Some people are like wolves in sheep clothing. They usually pretend to be nice or just want to give you a lift in their car, but they might have bad intentions. People can betray you, sell you out and leave you with nothing. It's hard to trust people. Many of us are really optimistic about other people, but not all people have good intentions. It's a lesson you have to learn in life. I know I did.

I have learned many lessons in my life, but the most valuable lesson was that my family is the most important thing I had. If you can trust your family members, you are a truly lucky person. I loved my family, my mom was a wonderful cook, and she used to prepare the tastiest bread I have ever eaten in my life. The bread was baked using the recipes passed on for generation to generation in the family and nothing in this life tasted as good. My father used to plow the fields and plant potatoes, rye, wheat, and other crops. We had lots of wonderful animals: cows, horses, chickens, ducks, and pigs. We had to put a real effort to survive through the winter. All year long, we had to work hard to prepare for the cold winter season. There was no question of whether we should help our parents or not because it was a question of survival; if we didn't help our relatives and neighbors, then we would have no food or wood for the winter and we could die from cold and starvation. Fresh bread and a cup of milk was the most important thing in our life. Sometimes a lump of bread is more priceless than gold. You should remember that. It might save your life someday.

My life had all the colors you could imagine. I liked nature, it inspired me. I loved the land, the fertile grounds, and the open fields. It was like a song for the young and curious. I loved the farm animals; they were the first best friends I had. I liked to rub the forehead of cows. Cows are wonderful domestic animals. I also liked to take care of the chickens, I would let them out in the field, look after them so they don't run away or get eaten by the foxes. Once I even taught a chicken to fly. Yes, I know that chickens don't fly, but I know that one did for sure. I took one chicken, held her in my hands and made her flap her wings by raising her up and lowering her down. I guess it's a natural bird instinct because she instinctively flapped her wings. After some time, the chicken started to fly over the fence. My mom wasn't really happy about that, so she cooked that flying chicken.

Every time I wanted to relax, I lay on the ground and gazed at the sky. It was so amazing. The sunlight, the fresh smell of cut grass, wheat and grain, the giant open fields that inspired my imagination, the wonderful weather and those sunbeams running through me; it felt magical. I was amazed by such wonders, like the clouds in the sky. Sometimes they reminded me of a wonderful carnival for spectators from all parts of the world. Everyone who had just a little bit of imagination could see the wonders in those clouds. Once, I saw the vanilla sky. The clouds were so beautiful like never before, they were in the soft tone of the red color. Sometimes I wondered how God created such a wonder like our world. All those animals, everything that swam, crawled and flapped their wings. It was such an amazing orchestra of color, beauty, magic, tunes, scents, and love.

Once I was sitting near a table with my mom, preparing dough for the bread and suddenly I wondered how God created the seas and land. Then my mom poured flour and water into the bowl, and in that moment, everything was clear to me. I was given a simple answer to a rather hard question. I had just asked for it in my mind and I received what I was asking for, instantly. That is the beauty of this world.

My life wasn't all perfect; like every family, my mom and dad had their own struggles. Every family has its own corners. That's just how life is. You can't live in perfect harmony; life isn't all blossoms, it has a few thorns in it too. My mom and dad used to argue. Work was hard and we didn't have lots of lands. We were not rich, but we lived near the lake, so after work, I would jump in, fully clothed, and watch the sunbeams reflecting off the shiny surface of the water. It was so beautiful and relaxing. I would calm down and just float on the surface of the water. It was so wonderful.

Sometimes, happiness is in the small things of life. Like the first breath of fresh air in the morning, the first drops of rain in spring, the first barefooted steps on the ground outside your home, your dog running around your feet and licking your hands when you reach for him, the fresh smell and taste of honey that has just been gathered from the hive, the taste of fresh milk from a cow, the refreshing sunlight through the day and the sunset on the horizon in the evening, Mom's freshly baked pastry, the new shoes dad got you from the store. There are so many wonders in this life, but you don't see them all. You run past them from your home on the way to work. We don't see the beauty all around us, the wonder that surrounds us all. The gift we are given by God to us. That gift is called life and we forget it, day after day. You run after things you don't need in the life you don't live. I know most people do this, but look where you stand now. Your resources are exhausted every day; poverty is a major issue, even when your civilization has the food to feed all of the people of Earth. Greed, fear and new walls between people are growing faster and faster. You hide in your rooms, from a world that is more magical and wonderful than everything you have ever seen. You hide behind your technology and live only in the imaginary world. But how long will your fantasy last? Probably until somebody pulls a cord and you fall back into reality, scaring you like a small rabbit. But hopefully, after some time, you will realize that reality is more precious than any fantasy or imagination land you have been living in.

If you think you are small and not worth the wonders of this life, you are wrong. The only wall standing between you and your dreams is your low self-confidence and low self-esteem. You think your life is hard and unfair. You think your mind is empty and your muscles are weak. So train your mind, lift your self-esteem and build up yourself, to the best you can be, because nobody else will do it for you. Nobody else will come into your life and train your brain, your muscles, find you a perfect mate for life, climb your first big mountain and fulfill your dreams. We all have our own way, but you must remember that, sometimes, the road gets hard and you want to drop everything. It's in those moments that we build our strength, in those moments we fight our weakness and carry on. Those moments separate the weak from the strong and in those moments, we reach our biggest potential.

Sometimes I come back from the fields, exhausted from work and tired as hell, but I always went to sleep right away on my bed and dream the most beautiful dreams I could imagine; beautiful flowers, the small waves crashing on the shore of a lake and my parents looking after me. Everything is wonderful in those dreams and I am happy. My childhood was perfect, with all the hard work, abraded arms and dirty barns. I was never happier.

I always wanted to know what's on the other shore of the big lake where I lived. So one day, I took a horse and rode near the shore of the lake. I saw wonderful places and many different people who were friendly and in good spirits, who helped me to continue on my adventure. I was very thankful for that. It took me a few hours, but finally, I was on the other side of the shore. I could see my house. It was a wonderful adventure. I fell on the ground, happy. It was so fulfilling that I had achieved something big. I was proud of myself. I was finally really happy. I looked into the sky and the clouds. It was so magical, like looking for a life of new possibilities and hope. I closed my eyes and just wanted to forget the whole world. I could hear the birds, my horse eating the grass. I was already falling asleep when someone put their hands on my eyes. I was startled, but I gently took those hands off. It was a beautiful girl, with a ring of flowers on her head, made from yellow flowers gathered in the field. I had never seen someone as beautiful as she was. She had hair so white, it could reflect the sunbeams; she was like an angel who was sent from heaven.

"Hello," I said.

"Hello." She replied.

"Who are you?"

"I'm Ieva."

"It's a beautiful name."

"Thank you. What are you doing in our field?"

"Sorry. I didn't know it's yours." I replied.

"Relax. I'm just teasing you."

"Ok. Thanks."

"Who are you?"

"I'm Jonas," I answered.

"What a great name. Where are you from?"

"I'm from the other side of the lake."

"Oh, I see. You know how the lake is called?" She asked.

"I think it's Lukstas."

"You know what it means?"

"Yes, it means a shell of the egg." I quipped.

"I think we all have a shell."

"Really?"

"Yes. But some of us break the shell and others carry that shell through their whole life."

Those were the most profound words I had ever heard. Then suddenly, she leaned over and kissed me. Her kiss was soft and warm, like a fresh breath of air in the morning. I was in the clouds, she was wonderful and we were both young. We met with each other as often as we could. She reminded me of someone I used to know, a long time ago. It was like the meeting of spirits that were separated a long time ago. I was as happy as she was. We used to talk about everything. Our parents got a little mad because we never used to do our work at home and her parents didn't like me much. They always told us we were too young. We used to relax in the fields and just talk for hours and hours. She became my closest friend. When the sky turned dark we used to look into the sky and watch the stars shining in the endless space of the cosmos.

"What do you think is there?" She asked.

"I don't know why do you ask?"

"I don't know, I'm just thinking. Are there people like us, looking to in the sky like we are?"

"I have no idea. I guess there could be something, but we probably would never know. Why do you ask these questions?"

"In school, there is a teacher who said that there are different planets in our solar system and you can view them from a telescope. But sadly we don't have one." She said.

"The only thing we have in the entire village is a radio," I replied.

"Yes, but it would be great to have a telescope."

"I guess it would."

We used to talk like this on and on. We talked about animals, about farming, how our days went, what we learned in school. It was wonderful, I really found a good friend.

Life went on. Her parents didn't like me much, because at that time there was lots of work to be done and spending time with me wasn't really their plan, but we met a few times in the week anyway. She was so wonderful and had many ideas and wanted to travel, she was really beautiful and intelligent. Talking to her made me feel like a better person, she had a spark of life and everybody who knew her thought she was a wonderful person. We tried to spend more time together despite the fact that her parents didn't like the idea that much. We were happy together. I guess that was love, a young and careless love. When you feel such love, you want the other person to be happy no matter what. Such love completes you, makes you a good person and fills your heart with compassion for others. Many people only dream about such things. We were really happy and had a careless life.

NEW CHAPTER

But like all wonderful stories, they always have an end. We heard about the German occupation and the invasion of the Soviet Union. We would never have imagined that those new German and Soviet powers would determine the future of our country. When the Germans seized power over Lithuania, they started transporting Jews to concentration camps or just dug giant graves and executed them. They didn't spare women or children. It was a horrible time for many people because many others who were not happy with the government were sent to death camps or work camps. In work camps, people didn't last long either. The harsh conditions for many were a death sentence. Lithuania was a small country and we hadn't much choice. Germans or Soviets, there was little difference, because either one or the other, they just wanted us on our knees.

When the war started, one of my brothers went to the war for the German side. He had no choice; he was conscripted and that meant he had to serve in the Nazi army. My mother cried all night long because she knew that he would never come back. The Germans pressed forward towards Soviet territory, but they were stuck. The Soviet troops fought with their last breath and turned the tide of the war.

I was about 20 years old. The Soviets pressed harder and pushed the Germans back. The Nazi army had no choice but to retreat. In a few months, Lithuania was under Soviet occupation and it was back to the same song again. Many people were under pressure from the Soviets: teachers, doctors, and wealthy peasants were sent to Siberia by train. A signature from the head of the KGB, Beria, meant only one thing; a ticket to the uninhabited work camps in Russia. Siberia was a horrible place for those who were born in Lithuania, Latvia, Estonia, Poland, Ukraine, Belarus, and Russia. There was no exception made for women, children and old people. That was no concern for the First Secretary of the Soviet Union, Joseph Stalin. He was the heartless leader of the USSR who sent millions of people to their final destination, where only a few survived. Some people were smart; they hid a few potatoes in their clothes and when they reached Siberia they planted them and from the small harvest, they survived through the horrible winter season. The differences between Hitler and Stalin were minimal. They were both madmen, only the craziness was different. One was a socialist, the other a nationalist.

The Second World War, for many people, ended on 2 September 1945, but in the Soviet Union, things were different. Many men hid

in the woods and fought in the partisan movement. Usually, they were
the only way for the people to survive through the Soviet invasion. The
Forest Brothers were the only ones who helped people fight the Soviets.
People fed the Forest Brothers, gave them food and helped however
they could. Sometimes, the Soviets executed whole villages of people.
The Soviets sent people suspected of helping the Forest Brothers to
Gulags, the same way Nazis sent people to death camps. So the quiet
war in Eastern Europe continued. The fighting went on for years. The
radio was full of messages claiming that the USA will soon attack the
Soviet troops in the Baltics, but that never happened and many people
hidden in the forests were left on their own. The most horrible fate was
reserved for those who supported the Forest Brothers or didn't join the
Soviet Army. They were usually tortured and prosecuted and sentenced
to death or sent to Siberia. I was one of those people.

It was a beautiful morning and the sun was shining brighter than
ever. I was happy because it was the day my mother usually baked bread
and her bread always tasted wonderful. It was so warm and tasty that
day and I will never forget the taste. Suddenly, I heard the sound of a
truck. Someone disembarked from the truck and knocked on our door.
That day and the face of that KGB officer will forever be burned in my
memory.

"Open up." The KGB officer demanded.

"What do you want?" My mother asked.

"Your son John is about 20 year's right?"

"You are right." My father replied.

"Time to join the glorious Soviet army," the officer declared.

"Please, no," my mother begged.

"I have no time for this, John, come with me."

"But my brother is in the German army, how can I shoot
my brother?" I protested.

"I don't care."

Mother fell on her knees, begging the officer to leave her son, but the officer just hit her. I couldn't watch that and hit the officer back. It was the biggest mistake I ever made in my life.

"You bastard. That will cost you." He snarled.

I remember a few soldiers taking me to the truck and driving me to an unknown location. The next 7 days were the most horrible of my entire life. They took me to the KGB headquarters located in Vilnius. I was taken downstairs in the cellar, where many people were often tortured and executed. They put me in a room and beat the hell out of me. They wanted to make me confess something I didn't do and I knew that if I had signed the paper they gave me, they would execute me the same day so I tried to hold out for as long as I could. Three KGB officers beat me every day and took me to a red room where there was no place to lay. I had to stand all the time while the red light was shining in my eyes and making me dizzy. One day, they had some type of wire around my neck and squeezed it as hard as they could. They shouted at me to put my signature on the paper before me. They shouted and dropped me on the floor. One of the KGB officers put his boot on my face and yelled at me to put my signature on the paper. They knew it was a death sentence for me if I did it. Finally, after beating me for several hours, they were tired and put me in the red room. This cycle of torture and pain lasted for 7 days. On the last day, they dragged me out and put something over my head and marched me through a corridor. It felt horrible; I thought that was the last day of my life. My whole life flashed through my head. The journey through those corridors was endless; they screamed and shouted at me. Every step of the way, I felt fear because, with every step, I could get a bullet in the head. I felt the air flowing through my body and every corridor was like an endless road to my last destination. They usually took out the gun and shoot the victims at the back of the head. I knew this and every step was making my life flow by slowly, like in a movie.

They kicked me and beat me all the way. They dragged me outside and into a truck. There were more people like me on the vehicle. One of them was really scared and shouted through the whole journey. I thought they were transporting us to our final destination. Then the truck stopped. Officers got us out and took the bags off our heads. They always shouted, urging us to hurry and move along. It was a train station. At that moment, I realized we were going to live because there were many people who were transported on the train wagons. There were women and children, elderly people, even sick people. They put us inside the cattle wagons. Everybody was scared and they didn't know what awaited them. But I was certain; they were transporting us to Siberia. The troopers had dogs and guns. They always shouted at us to hurry.

"Bistrey, bistrey (faster, faster)."

It was a nightmare filled with many scared and broken people. Children crying, mothers weeping, people from all over the country were there. Millions of innocent people from all over the Soviet Union were sent to Siberia, they were hungry, scared and lost. It was a real hell and the devil of this horror had only one name: Joseph Stalin. That monster could append one signature and doom thousands or even millions of people. It was a horror of unknown proportions. Lithuania, Latvia, Estonia, Poland, Belarus, Ukraine; every former Soviet country would suffer the same fate. Mass deportations to Siberian gulags were a norm and millions suffered this horrific fate. Those families who had someone enlisted in the Red Army or working for the Soviets were considered lucky and even then, their fate was hanging in the balance. The most horrible fate was reserved for those who were richer or had more land. Soviets gave their land to the poor, taking the property from the rich and deporting them to Siberian work camps. Usually, that was a final destination for many men, women, children, especially the elderly who had no chance of survival. The Red Army didn't even allow people to bury the dead. The ones who survived will never forget that hell they came through.

I was lucky that time, viciously beaten, but still alive. I dragged myself to one of the cattle wagons. Every bone in my body hurt like hell. I was suffering from unbearable pain throughout my whole body. My head was hurting from insomnia in the red room, but I was alive and that was the most important thing. I was certain that today was the last day of my life, but God probably had a different plan for me. I fell on the floor. Some old lady helped me and put some hay under my head and I fell asleep. I didn't hear the screams and cries anymore, just the emptiness and the void flowing in my head. I dreamt of the girl I met on the other shore of the lake. We were running in the open fields; there were no trains, no Red Army, nothing that could hurt us. It was a magical dream. She always smiled at me; we kissed, swam in the water of the lake, fell in the hay and just looked into the clouds. Then I woke up to reality. The place was tight; many people were put into the cattle wagons. Some were scared, some were desperate, others just cried. There was a small girl who couldn't stop crying, I tried to calm her down. She smiled when she looked at me and I smiled back. She was scared and told me that she lost her parents. I hugged her and told her that everything would be fine and that we would get through this. There were lots of scared people who were looking at me, asking me where we were going. I would have been glad to tell them, but I simply didn't know. The destination was uncertain and many people were just scared. I wanted to calm them down and tell them it would be alright, but deep in my heart, I knew that many of those people wouldn't survive. I wasn't certain of my fate either.

My whole body hurt from the beatings of the KGB officers, but still, I was alive. I hoped I would survive this and I hoped that in the end, the destination of the journey would be more pleasant. But at that time, we were just people in the cattle wagons who, one way or another, were scared like never before. Many things at that time were uncertain and many things were hidden; only your grandparents who survived can tell the truth. I knew only one thing, that people in such hard conditions should help each other as much as they can.

People told stories of how Russian soldiers entered villages; they took away people who had more land than others, the ones who were educated or just simply the ones who they didn't like. They raped women in front of their husbands, took children away from their mothers, and killed anyone who didn't obey. Somebody joined the resistance in forests, somebody joined the Soviets, somebody betrayed their brothers or sisters, children betrayed their parents to the NKVD and parents sent their children to Siberia. One of those children survived and returned to Lithuania and wrote a book about her story. My only fault was that I didn't want to join the Soviet army. And now, I was one of those people who were on the train to the work camps in Siberia.

The sounds of people crying were horrible. Mothers, elderly, children, no one were spared. It was a time of despair, a time of horrible agony, a time of pain and a time of courage, a time of horror and a time of hope. I thought we would be executed and buried in some unknown grave where no one would ever find us. There were many people in the cattle coaches: children and mothers, elderly and young, sick and healthy. There were no differences; everyone was equal on that train. Some were teachers, others, doctors, some were just people who just wanted to be free. People were scared, they didn't know what awaited them; many people said that we would all be put in a concentration camp and executed. People were desperate and despaired; nobody knew what would happen next. We all prayed to live another day and our prayers echoed through the whole Soviet Union. People were cramped in small cattle carriages heading to some unknown destination. We were all like family there, scared of the future and the horrors that awaited us, but talked to each other and encouraged each other that no matter what happens, we would survive through this.

If you are feeling scared and lost and somehow you feel there is no hope, don't worry, there is always hope. Hope never dies, because there is God and he is watching us from heaven and will judge those who do evil and those who do good. He will give strength to the weak and take away strength from those who are too strong. And no matter what you do, always trust God and know that there is a road hidden from you that you don't yet understand, but God has a plan for you and this plan will keep you strong and will only make sense in the future. I imagined my future, living with my family and that image and dream kept me going through the hardest times I endured the Siberian winters. The image of this wonderful family kept me on my feet when I fell down many times, over and over again. I imagined that this family will be with me and that image of hope and my future wife and daughter would be the only thing that would be important for me in the future. That spark kept me sane and kept my mind in check.

I saw a small girl who was scared and was holding her mother's hand as tightly as she could. I asked her how she felt. She just moved closer to her mother looking lost and scared. I wanted to cheer her up. I wanted her to stop crying so much, so I told her a story about a prince in a big castle that lived in a faraway land. And that in this place we were heading, there would be beautiful lands, lots of good people and lots of new friends she would meet. I told her that there would be lots of horses, cows, and chickens. I wanted her to feel safe and wanted her to know that everything would be good and she would find a magical place to live her life with someone who was kind and would treat her well. I told her that she would live in a safe home and will have lots of friends who will love her just the way she is and she would have all her dreams come true. I talked to her mother and she felt calmer about their future. I took her hand and held her for some time. I wanted her to feel safe and hopeful about the future. Many people were scared because they didn't know what was awaiting them. Neither did I. I was viciously beaten, hungry, desperate and on a train in cattle wagons sent to the unknown destination. There were many of us. The only thing we knew was that we had to survive. We all felt that we needed to come through this because if we didn't, history would forget us. The nights in those smelly and dirty wagons will stick in my memory forever. Nobody knew what awaited us and where we would be dropped off. The only thing I knew was that I had to survive these conditions and tell the story about those horrible events to my children and grandchildren.

The only thing I knew for certain was to be quiet about politics because people were scared and the last thing we needed was to discuss who was worse, Hitler or Stalin. I understood one thing; they were like the two sides of one coin, both evil and hungry for power.

The journey was getting long, my bones were still hurting, my harshly beaten body felt heavy. I could stand, but my feet felt weaker and weaker. I almost forgot my bleeding nose and my hard beaten body. The body always heals faster than the mind. I wanted to rest on the ground, but I couldn't because there were women and children who needed more rest than me. The place was cramped, we all were tired, but something kept us strong. Some old lady started singing. The song was the most beautiful song I had ever heard.

Lithuanian:
　　MARIJA, Marija, Skaisčiausia Lelija,
　　Tu Motina mūsų šalies,
　　Pagelbėk lietuviui,
　　Palengvink mūs būvį,
　　Išgelbėk nuop riešo baisaus...
　　Mes ašarom plūstam, vergijoje žūstam!
　　Marija, maldos išklausyki
　　Prieš mūsų bedievius,
　　Lietuvių engėjus

Visus mus vienybėn suglausk!

Tik Tu Užtarėja, tik Tu mūs Gynėja,
Marija, Marija šventa,`

Išmelsk pas Augščiausią,
Dievulį geriausią
Mums laisvę brangios Lietuvos.
English:
MARIJA, Mary, the Brightest Lily,
You Mother of our country,
Help every Lithuanian,
Make it easier for us
Save us from the fearsome enemy.
We are full of tears, dying in slavery!
Mary, listen to our prayer
Save us from our godless enemies,
Lithuanian oppressors
Let unite us all!

Only you are our savior, Only You are our Defense,
Mary, holy, Mary
Pray for us to the Lord,

God the merciful
Give freedom for us and our dear Lithuania.

We all started to sing. We felt this wonderful feeling of unity and solidarity with each other. We felt like we belonged to something greater. The other coaches were singing too. We felt like the whole country was singing with us and it was, only that I never saw it. Lithuania became independent on March 11th 1990, soon after Latvia and Estonia declared their independence on May 4th, 1990 and August 20th, 1991.

You wonder what happened. How I died? What became of my dreams? You just have to read the whole book to understand the full story.

Independence is one of the most important things a country or even a person could have. If a person is bound to circumstances such as sex trade or sweatshop work, or being a political prisoner or prisoner of war or being persecuted because of gender, race or sexual orientation. All those things make a person empty, lost and looking for something most of you take for granted because you live in an age of prosperity and the only important thing you have to think about is which iPhone to buy. In many countries, life isn't that easy. People have to fight for bread and water, people have to struggle in poverty and many live in conditions of war and prosecution. If you live in a prosperous country, you have to thank God that you do.

Where did I trail off? Oh yes, the train. We were headed to Siberia. I only discovered that much later. At first, we were all scared like never before, but with time, we accepted our fate and decided that whatever happens, we all will be strong and try to survive everything that comes at us.

When the weather got colder, we understood we were headed north. We knew the children were vulnerable so we gave some of our clothes to keep the children warm. Through the bars, we could see the cold Russian countryside. There were few people, probably because many were scared of the oppressions and didn't want to get in the way of the government. In time, I understood that many Russians are good people, but the corrupt Soviet regime and heads of the communist party are truly evil and even a danger to their own people. Many Russians where exiled, tortured and killed when communists seized power in Russia. The lucky ones escaped in time, but for the ones who didn't, the name Soviet Union became hell on earth. Before the revolution, Russia had one of the leading economies in Europe. After, it was in ruins. For us, the people of oppressed countries like Lithuania, Estonia, Latvia and Poland, the horrors were just starting. Many of us were sent to work in camps all over the Soviet Union and Joseph Stalin's favorite destinations were in Siberia. Climates there are unimaginably cold in the wintertime.

We had horrible clothes, they were intended for warmer Lithuanian climates, but not for the cold weathers of Siberia. My bones started to feel numb and my muscles started to feel the pain from cold of Siberian weather. We all gathered the children to the center to make them feel warmer and took them inside the warm cocoon to make them warmer. Nobody wanted the children to get cold. Elderly people were also in the middle of the cocoon made from our bodies. We knew we had to survive, whatever it took. That was the most important; thing to protect the children and the elderly because they couldn't protect themselves.

Sometimes, in your life, you have to understand that you are not the most important person in the world. You have to mind and take care of other people. The most important person isn't sitting inside your head, the most important people are your children, your spouse, your parents and many other people you are related to or connected with. After all, we are all connected with one another. We are linked like smartphones in a giant high-speed superhighway internet and our actions reflect on others. If we hurt one person, we hurt the whole world, because if there is someone weaker, smaller, older or disabled and we forget about them in our cold hearts, we become distant from God and He surely will punish us for that. Everything we do or we don't do reflects in our future, like in a small mirror we see in front of us. A small and generous action or a good intention could create a whole new chain of events that will shine through for us in the future. Many people think that a small thing will never impact their lives. They are wrong. On the train, something happened. I will remember it for the rest of my life. When I was young I saw a small bird with a broken wing on the road. I brought the bird home and tried to heal it. After some time taking care of that bird, I realized that caring for others is the most important thing to do. But the most wonderful thing was that, in that train, when we all were desperate, scared and lonely, a lone bird of the same kind flew inside the train wagon. He flew in to my hands. The children were so interested that they forgot about the cold and the horrible conditions inside the train. They touched the bird and looked happier than if they had just received a piece of bread. In that moment, I understood that everything I thought I knew about the world was wrong, that whatever happens, I must survive this trip and most importantly, return to Lithuania. Even if it would cost my life I must die, in my land. I must be there where I belong. That was my pledge to myself and it became my destiny.

After some time, the train stopped. One of the officers had a list; he called some names and the ones who were on the list had to come out. The soldiers ordered women and children from the train. The women screamed and held their children tighter to their bodies, but the soldiers were harsh and cold. They had no feelings and just waved their guns, ordering everyone around. They were cold as steel and harsh as stone. They had no feelings for the poor and frightened people. They were like people in slaughterhouses, pushing the animals out of the cow carriages. I didn't know what happened to those women and children, maybe they were sent to work camps, and maybe they were fitted inside homes alongside good people. I don't know because I wasn't there. I only know that was the time our roads were separated and I was headed deeper into Siberian forests.

I didn't know why, but somehow my feet were shivering. I was scared like never before, somehow I felt what was coming. My body felt numb, I felt goose bumps all over my body. All my senses were alert. I didn't know what to expect next. I knew exactly that after my detention, the red room, the angry soldiers nearly beating me to death,

I had only a few other options. The first option was that they would execute me the next time I step out of the train, the next was that I would be sent to a death camp or a work camp. Another option was that I would soon be sitting at a table with Joseph Stalin and he would apologize to me for all the trouble. Yes, I hadn't lost my sense of humor even in such conditions. I even told a joke to the people who were with me. Some of them laughed, some didn't, somebody even cried. I knew one thing: whatever happened I must get through this, no matter what. After all, somebody has to tell my story.

After some time, the train stopped. There were soldiers shouting, ordering everybody from the train. We thought it was our time; the soldiers put everyone in a row and ordered us to follow them. They waved their guns and pushed us deeper inside the forest. The road became harder and harder and we felt the cold through our bodies. We were shivering from the cold pain inside our bones. Our feet hurt and our clothes weren't appropriate for the climate. Some of us fell to the ground and the soldiers just kept on beating the ones who couldn't walk. There were elderly people, they were scared and if this had continued, I knew they had no chance for survival. After a five hour walk, we stopped. I thought this was it. It was the moment we were all going to die. My feet shivered and my hands were cold but I held my whole strength to stand tall. I closed my eyes and remembered my youth, those open green fields, that wonderful smell of fresh milk, the loving hands of my mother, the smile on my father's face. Everything seemed so clear and so bright, I thought we were all going to die that day. I heard the soldiers shouting and screaming at us, but I didn't care I was lost to time and lost to this world. I felt the warmth in my hands and couldn't hear the sounds anymore. I started to pray and wanted that this to end quickly, so I could be closer with my mother and my father back in heaven where we all could be together.

Suddenly, I felt a blow on my face with a rifle. A soldier had hit me with his gun. I fell on the ground. Next, he gave me the object in his hands and showed me to the nearest tree. It was an ax and then I understood everything; he wanted me to cut down trees. I returned to reality. I was relieved that I wasn't going to die today. The forest was full of people like me. We were ordered to work somewhere in Siberia where we had to cut down trees and load them to the trucks, where they were taken to some unknown location. The work was hard, my hands hurt and some of us fell on the ground. The pain from the cold made our hands freeze, after some time, our hands felt like wooden sticks, but we had to work because if we didn't, we would freeze to death. You have to understand that the most important thing in such conditions was the need to work because if you didn't your muscles would atrophy, you would fall down and might never get back again. That was the most important lesson I learned that day because some people fell down and were taken somewhere, so I had to keep on. I had to continue to work, even if my whole body hurt from the intense work, my feet were cold and my hands felt numb.

Another person fell on the ground; he seemed so weak and desperate, I had to help him. I helped him up and asked him to continue the work because if he didn't, his fate would be sealed. He took his ax and we both kept on chopping the tree next to us. I tried to help him as much as I could, but he was very weak. I helped him as much as I could, but nothing was easy for us that day. The cold was horrible, we both felt like we were giving our best that day. Muscles were hurting; our fingers almost froze to the ax. But we carried on. The day felt like it would never end, our hands felt numb from the cold and our feet hurt from carrying the giant trees to the trucks. Nothing was easy that day, but I was still alive, I was breathing and my strength grew more and more that day. I don't know what was driving me. Maybe it was the will to live, or maybe the strong Lithuanian blood that was in my veins and wanted to prove something to myself, or maybe it was just pride in my head that told me that I had to survive this.

The sun was going down and the soldiers took us to some cabins. The cabins had wooden beds, so we all fell in them. Those hard wooden beds felt like feather beds. The cold was unimaginable. But we fell asleep anyway. That night, I had strange dreams. My father was calling to me in my dreams, some Soviet soldiers took him. I shouted, but they took him anyway.

I woke up from the horror. I looked to the left. There was an old man beside me. I wanted to wake him up, but he was cold and suddenly I understood he was dead, I looked to the right there was another man about my age, but he didn't move, I tried to wake him up, but he was still and cold as stone. At this moment, I understood that I may never come back from this place and I could die here all alone. But I wouldn't give up so easily. I knew that I had to survive.

The next morning, the soldiers took us to chop the trees again. I did my best. I knew the only thing that was saving me was the hard work that kept me warm, so I continued. There were some prisoners who seemed to be more favored by the guards. The guards even gave them cigarettes to smoke; they were called thieves in law. They were criminals who had special privileges and hated people like me, they hated the political prisoners. One of them came to me and started to laugh and insult me. I knew that if I resisted he would beat me, so I just kept on doing my work. He insulted me, laughed at me and spat on me, but after a while, he was bored and went off to find another victim.

Some soldiers threw a piece of bread to us prisoners; we all jumped in and filled our stomachs with a few lumps of bread. I was tired as hell and later that night, I fell on the hard wooden bed like a stone on the ground. That night was like none before it. I had strange dreams of people calling me, and somehow I felt that those people were dead. They all called me to some tunnel and that tunnel seemed to never end and I was really scared. Suddenly, I woke up all covered in sweat. It was the scariest dream I had in my life.

A new day had come and it was time to work. Soldiers pushed us around. People were so exhausted from work, some of them fell on the ground. The ones who were lucky continued to chop wood. Sometimes your body gets so tired, you can't feel yourself. It is very hard to go on, but you just gather your strength and do one thing at a time. Just try to go on as far you can, because nobody else will do it for you. Nobody will understand your weakness and your weakness could mean the end of you.

The cold was horrible; our feet and fingers felt like wood; they were slowly getting blue. You had to go on because only work saved you. That hard work that kept you alive was the only thing that mattered. All the blood rushed through my veins like wildfire, I felt sweat going through my body. I was exhausted but I carried on. The only thought in the mind was: "I have to survive, no matter what it takes." I wanted to help others too. It was important to have an open mind and help others. If you are alone, you are weaker and more vulnerable. I helped other prisoners to stand up and continue the work. They seemed desperate, but I cheered them on because we all needed to continue our work, we all needed to keep going on and the only thing that could keep us safe and warm was the chopping of those God-damned trees in the middle of nowhere.

That day, they sent me to another barracks. There was a criminal gang in that barrack. They were called thieves in law. They were the highest class of the prisoners and even some soldiers respected them. One of them had two stars tattooed on his left and right shoulder, meaning he had a higher status in the criminal society. He came up to me and started laughing at me and hitting me on the head. He quickly understood that I was a political prisoner and criminals didn't have even the slightest respect for us. He took off his fur coat called a *vatinka* and showed the tattoo of Stalin on his chest. He used to swear and hit me all the time. He also invited his friends to join him. They were beating me as hard as they could. One blow, then another. They tried their best to clobber me with everything they got. I felt my leg break. The pain was immeasurable but they didn't stop. I tried to protect my head with my hands, but they continued. They broke some of my fingers too. One time, I thought they had stopped and just gave up. But one of them took a wooden stick and broke my hand when I tried to protect my head. Then finally, I fell unconscious.

NEW CHAPTER

I woke up somewhere in the woods. My hand hurt, but my leg hurt even more. I couldn't crawl very well but I tried to do it as best I could. I didn't know where I was, but there was someone else lying on the ground. I gathered my strength and tried to reach that man. I crawled, braving the most horrible pain I have ever felt, I gathered my strength to be next to that man. I shouted at him, but he didn't move. He was still, like a stump of wood. Finally, I reached him. His face was blue and he wasn't breathing. He was dead. I said a prayer for him and closed his dead eyes with my fingers with my unbroken hand with healthy fingers. The other was broken and I couldn't move some of my fingers that were horribly injured. Near me, there was a forest. I saw a few trees and wanted to get close to them. I gathered my last strength and started to crawl. The pain was excruciating and my broken leg felt almost dead; it reminded me of a piece of wood and I already believed that if I got out of this, I would never have my leg back. I started coughing. The cold was finally getting to my lungs. I wanted to reach the trees to get away from the cold Siberian wind. The cough was getting really deep. I was coughing my lungs out so hard, I thought I would die. Finally, I dragged myself to the trees.

The pain was unimaginable and the cough was horrible. My chest was convulsing from coughing and my stomach was going mad from hunger. I knew I had to do something. So I did what I had to do. I dug up the snow and put some grass in my mouth. I knew it was cold and had pieces of dirt on it, but I had to do it because I wanted to survive. The grass was decent food but I was tired and couldn't crawl anymore. I garnered my strength to peal up some tree bark from the tree that I faced. The tree bark was hard and tasteless, but it had some value for my stomach. Hours passed and my cough was getting worse and the grass was getting more tasteless. I ran through my whole life. I remembered my youth and my family; I was probably dissipating and couldn't understand anything. I fell on the ground and couldn't feel anything. My eyes were shut down, my breath was getting weaker and I started to fade away slowly. I saw my whole life passing through, I remember it was like I was running in the empty fields of ray. I remembered the warmth of my mother's body when she was holding me in her arms; it was an amazing feeling. I started to lose myself slowly. The vision in my eyes began to fade and I didn't know what to do. What could I do, my life was slipping away from me. But one thought never left my mind. I wanted to die in my country. I thought God, please let me die in my country. I don't want anything else, just please let me die at home. I couldn't feel my legs. I couldn't feel my hands either. I knew it was over.

But then someone took me from the tree. I felt someone dragging my body. This is it I thought; now he will bury me. I couldn't fathom where he was dragging me, but I knew that this was my end; I would end up in some pit with dead men all next to me. I would surely die that day. Suddenly, I felt that I was being dragged into some home. He took me to a hard wooden bed and dropped some firewood into the fireplace. I was feeling awful, but he gave me a cup of hot water. After some time, my hands were feeling better. My vision was blurry, but I started to see some little things around me.

It was a small wooden home. It had a fireplace, a bed, and a small table with a kerosene lamp. He held up my head and gave me a cup of hot tea with some medical herbs. I didn't know what those herbs were, but they made me feel better. That man was trying to save me. He spoke Russian, but I didn't understand a word. I had to learn his language, little by little. I knew it was important. But the man was educated and knew some Lithuanian. He asked me what parts of me hurt. He asked about my country. Then he said the most important thing that I will always remember. Those words will stick with me to the end of my days. He said: I will save you, but you will have to save others. My bones were fractured but he put wooden sticks and bandages around my broken leg. I was feeling very bad, my cough wasn't going anywhere and I was really cold. My fever kept rising at nights and I was very tired from the pain. I knew that my friend who helped me was trying his best to save me, but my fever was really getting to me. I even lost consciousness a few times and woke up screaming from the horrors from my memories. I remembered the criminal with Stalin's tattoos on his chest. I tried to relax as much as I could. I knew that they were only nightmares, but I had to calm myself down because if I didn't, I would never make it home. The wish was a fantasy, I knew that I would probably never get back because the communist regime would never allow a political prisoner to escape the gulags of Siberia. Stalin and KGB Secretary Beria would never allow that.

The days went on, my cough was horrible, and it felt like I had been smoking a pack of cigarettes every day of my entire life. My friend gave me vodka from time to time; it eased the pain a little, but the taste was horrible, at that time I decided that I would never drink vodka again; it was such a horrible thing, it burned my mouth and made me vomit.

After a few weeks, the coughing improved, but my leg and hand were not so good. My friend invited a local Siberian woman to help me. She looked like an Eskimo or an Asian. She used to bring firewood and take care of me. I felt much better whenever she was around. She was a good person in her heart and she really helped me to slowly recover. She was a local herbalist and made me some tea from the herbs she found in the fields. She had a warm touch and really took good care of me. I was getting better day by day, but I couldn't walk like I used to. The broken leg really hurt; from time to time the leg showed me its weak points. I knew that life wasn't easy; I had to help the people that helped me. I knew that was my calling. Many things were new to me. This place was strange with all sorts of different people. Many of them were good in heart and I tried to help them as best as I could. Sometimes, in the night, I prayed to return to the land where I was born. I knew that my roots were important. The people here were also kind; they helped me overcome the hard truth that I may never walk again, but after all, I had hope, my hope was to return home, to the only place where I was needed and loved. Home was the most important thing for me. After all, those people were very different from the ones I was used to. Winters here were colder and the horrible pain in my left leg was getting me down. I knew that the important things like my family members and my future depended on my will to carry on and go further.

Family is the most important thing in life. Sometimes family is the people who surround us and we must do everything in our strength to carry on and help the ones who are close to us. Sometimes, we can't walk or just can't do some things, but we must try our best to help the ones who are close. Mother Teresa once said that first, we must help the ones who are close to us. Sometimes even prayer helps. But most importantly, when you help others, you help yourself. Serving other people is the greatest good we can achieve and nothing else in this world is more important. You must understand that nothing in this life is as good or as evil as only we used to see it. It doesn't mean we must walk away from evil. People who walk away from evil and do nothing are evil themselves. Jesus said it very clearly in the parable of the Good Samaritan.

Many times, I helped people; many times I gave them good advice. I knew that people started to respect me more. I helped people with advice and just with small little works here and there, many things turned out fine and the people who I helped seemed very helpful. They didn't want anything in return and I felt really embarrassed, they helped a cripple like me but didn't get anything back.

Sometimes, I dreamt about my country and those wonderful empty fields of grass and wheat. I dreamt about my past and sometimes, in some strange way, I dreamt of my future. I dreamt about a girl that was so beautiful and kind that I could never imagine it in real life. She seemed so fair and wonderful that I couldn't sleep anymore. I knew that somehow, I had to return to my country and my small little village near a lake. I couldn't understand how those horrible events happened, how our country was invaded and crushed in such a short time. We had an army, we had people who were opposing the strong hand of Stalin, but still, we were occupied and sent to Siberia in the hundreds of thousands. But we had a strong will and we all wanted to return to our homeland. That was one will we all shared and we never gave up hope on returning home. I saw many desperate people who were crushed. But somehow we knew that we had to help each other, some people shared wood for heat, some people shared their food with each other, and we were all in the same boat. We knew that one way or another, we had to help each other because if we didn't, we would become animals, not people. The only difference between an animal and a human is that humans try to help each other. If we live only for money and pleasure, if we would only seek shiny new things, we wouldn't be better than animals. We can only be the ones who are, and help the ones who are, close. We won't find something in the faraway lands and far away worlds. The things we seek are always closest to us. We just have to see them. People look for treasures and seek something different, but the road differs, the further from home we get. The people everywhere are different and I always remembered my childhood farm where I grew up. Sometimes, I would remember it in my dreams and it would always fill me with joy and happiness. That picture of my land and all of my friends who I used to spend my free time stuck inside my mind for a long time. In my dreams, I used to play with my friends and their faces used to keep me warm at night.

The people helped me to survive those horrible moments and would bring me firewood and food. I tried to help the local people with advice and warm words and sometimes with a hard word if I had to. Mostly, I gave advice about farming and agriculture, ethics and personal life. People of the village respected me and listened to my advice. Slowly I started to feel my legs more and could move them better. Days went by and I started to walk slowly. I fell many times, but with the help of my savior, the good doctor, I could move with a stick that some good people made for me. When I was getting even better, I started to do nursing chores at the local clinic the doctor was running. The good doctor showed me the basics of medicine and I quickly learned a few medical tricks. I respected that man every step of the way and through helping him, I knew he was a good doctor, an honorable person, and the Hippocrates Oath wasn't just words for this man.

Days went by and we brought more and more people from the gulag. Those people were starving, beaten and cold. Sometimes we had to amputate a few fingers or even a whole leg or an arm. The things that I saw in that clinic were horrible. I heard terrible stories about beaten and tortured people. People had far worse stories than mine and one really touched my heart. There was a small boy, aged seven or eight, who came to us for help. He was cold and hungry, he told us his story. The Soviets captured him and sent him to Siberia because he put patriotic pamphlets on the walls of Kaunas. The boy said to me:

-Mister, help me, I am a Lithuanian.

I will always remember those words. How could anyone send a child to this place? Only someone inhuman can do that. He was only a child. He was skinny, cold, desperate, helpless and hungry. Somebody sent that child to an unknown, freezing, hell hole just for a few sheets of paper glued on the wall. If somebody could do that, it meant humanity had lost its way and there might be no way back from this. We gave him food and put him near the fireplace. All the time, he was staring into the fireplace like he was looking into an abyss. We also gave him some warm clothes. Then the boy asked us if we would throw him away as all the other people did. We knew we had to help him with what we could. We took him in and asked him to do some simple housework. He was glad to stay with us. One lady took care of the boy and treated him like her son. She just couldn't leave such a wonderful and good child. He helped us with everything he could. He was grateful to us for saving him like I was to the good doctor saved me. That day I understood my purpose in life as the doctor said to me: "I will help you, but you must help others."

In fact, our purpose in life is to help others. There is no greater purpose than helping the ones who are weaker than us and in need of our help. How can there be another purpose in life? Everyone is looking for pleasures and lives only for themselves, but somehow their life is getting nowhere. They become unhappy and unsatisfied because they have no purpose; they just go through life satisfying their needs and desires. The strong people who are determined and have a purpose always are full of life; they achieve great things and are welcomed by many people because they know the key. They have something bigger than themselves. They have a purpose in life and that purpose is to help others.

Days went on and on. I helped the doctor to heal the patients and many other tasks he assigned to me. I had my hands full all the time. There were many, many people we dragged from the woods and helped to regain their strength. But one patient caught my attention. I knew him from before. That person was the criminal who broke my leg and twisted my fingers. He was weak, probably because his own friends ditched him. When he gained his consciousness, he was scared when he saw me. I saw the fear in his eyes, but I knew I had to help him, it was my duty. His left leg was blue. It was gangrene. The doctor and I knew that if we didn't operate, he would be dead. We explained to him that we had to cut off his leg. He shouted at us, but after some time he understood that we were right. He agreed on the operation. We had very little sedatives so we gave him some vodka. We used a bone saw; he screamed and shouted the whole time. I tried to hold him with every bit of strength I had, but he was really strong and it was really hard. We gave him more vodka and he became more relaxed. We cut off his leg and burned the wound with hot metal to stop the bleeding. We put bandages on the wound and let him sleep for a while.

I was standing next to the man who hurt me so much. I knew that this moment would define my future. My face burned with anger and I felt horrible. My heart pounded; if we had a heart monitor in those days, it would clearly spike at 200 millimeters of mercury. A million things rushed through my head; I couldn't understand what was going on. But somehow, I knew that if, today I did something to a weak and helpless person, the next day someone would do that to me. I took an ax while my mind was screaming and my head was feeling lost. Somehow, my face felt hot and that anger in me burned, but after a while, I relaxed. I remembered my mother and father who would never forgive me for the things that I wanted to do. I remembered them and the warm feeling rushed through my body. Then I remembered the girl in my dream and somehow the vengeance didn't matter. I felt sorry for that man, he was weak and helpless and I could never hurt someone like that. That man tortured me, made me go through such horrors I could never imagine, but I forgave him. I understood that no matter what he did, he lays there on that bed, weak and broken. All his power, all his strength was gone, he was like a weak baby. He was a horrible person, but that didn't give me the right to do something so terrible to him. I didn't give him life, so I had no right to take it away from him. The doctor rushed into the room.

"Are you crazy?" The doctor asked

"Why?" I asked

"You wanted to kill this man?"

"I don't know."

"Why did you want to kill him?"

"He did the most horrible things to me," I replied.

"Yes, perhaps she did, but he is weak and broken now. You have to help him, not hurt him. "

"Why?"

"You promised me, remember?"

"Yes, I know I promised."

"You swore an oath to me," the doctor replied.

"Yes, I did."

"Your word can't be broken."

"Yes I know," I said.

"Now promise me that you will never hurt anyone and that you will not steal and take anything that doesn't belong to you."

My hands felt hot and I dropped the ax on the ground. I couldn't do anything bad from then on. I went outside and thanked God that I didn't do something horrible today. I loved nature. I looked outside. Everything had meaning. It was one of the most important lessons of my life. Through all my life, this was the most important thing I didn't do. While listening to the singing birds, I couldn't stop thinking. I never could forget the face of a beautiful girl that was in my mind in that dream. It mesmerized me. Something that was so distinctive from all the other people. She had beautiful, soft dark hair. She seemed like someone who could change my day and make all my troubles disappear. All my pain would vanish. She was so beautiful like none other in my life.

I went to my humble home and relaxed. At that time, I could only think of a few things. I had to feed the chickens in my garden and clean the pig pit. I could understand that most of the time I had to take care of the patients in the clinic. Some of them were sick, some of them were hurt and desperate. They wanted attention, they wanted to be loved and cared for. I had to help the doctor; after all, he saved my life twice. Sometimes, the most important things are the ones you don't do.

When I was young, there was a small bird I found on the ground, lying with a broken wing. I took the bird in my hands and took him home. He was so weak and restless and I didn't want to see him that way. I tried to heal him, little by little. His wing was so broken that I was afraid he wouldn't be able to fly anymore. I was scared and wanted to help him. Good people helped me take care of him. I gave him food. Looking after him made me feel better. I knew that somewhere, someone in heaven was looking after us like I was looking after this bird. It made me feel comfortable. I knew that anything in the world was possible because of that person looking after us. Somehow, it made sense and it was clear that I was always looked after. At that moment, that I was holding the ax, I knew that the doctor was sent from heaven to save me. He saved me from the biggest mistake of my life. There are people who are sent from God; they are the most important people in your life: parents, teachers, doctors, people who just wish you well. But the stick always has two sides, some people are sent from the devil. They are horrible people; if you meet such people, do your best to avoid them. Get away from them as fast as you can, because those people will poison your soul. Those individuals are broken inside, even if you try to reason with them, it's useless. People who are jealous and angry and are full of envy are people you should avoid. Those are the dictators, people angry at the whole world, people with no empathy of other people's pain, wolves in sheep clothing and the ones who pretend to be your friends but plot behind your back.

I tried to help the people in need; in the clinic and nursing home, I took care of the people, cleaned them and helped them walk. I rolled them in bed so they wouldn't feel left alone and empty, I did my best and that made me happy. It made sense because helping others is the best thing you can do, it fills up your soul with goodness and compassion. After all, we will all meet each other after death and God will judge us accordingly for every good thing and bad. Life is not easy, we make hard choices, but we must make them because if we don't, we would stand alone in emptiness and darkness. You have to respect your elders, you have to respect your parents, and you have to respect your kids and grandkids. There is a soul looking up to you in their eyes and they make you feel like you have someone important close to you. You have a precious gift; a gift of life and you shouldn't waste it on anger, judgment, resentment, bigotry, self-doubt, and evil. Many people think that the more they have, the happier they would be. So tell me, why are many billionaires so unhappy? Why are people in the slums of India always cheering and smiling? They have hope in their eyes; they have something that many people misunderstand. They are simply thankful for what they have. Many people think if they attain one thing in their life, it would make them happy -if they could get that new wonderful smartphone then they would be happy. Someone in China sold his kidney for a smartphone. Do you think that person is happy now? Helping others and working for the greater good is happiness. We must understand that.

NEW CHAPTER

The next day I went to the prisoner who hurt me. The doctor told me not to do anything stupid like I wanted to do. I sat near him. We talked for a bit. He told me his story; how his father beat him, how he gathered empty bottles in the streets and with the money from the bottles he brought bread for his mother and his two little sisters. His father wanted alcohol, but he didn't buy any for him. His mother died and his father threw him in the streets with his sisters. They hid in a decrepit apartment and he would steal food for his sisters. I felt sorry for that man. What he went through was horrible. Those were horrible times in Russia. People were shot for no reason, for the smallest things. Eventually, they all ended up in foster care. One of his sisters found a young officer. He was a good man and she was lucky. The other sister wasn't so lucky. She found a criminal who introduced his sister and him to a criminal life. A criminal life is very horrible with its rules and doctrine. The crime boss would hurt his sister, until one day he had enough. He bought a gun from the black market and shot the crime boss when he was beating his little sister. After that, there was no rest in his life. He had to show his authority against other gang members to protect his sister from them. He killed some of those people. But the nightmares of those days haunted him every night. Every night, he saw their faces running after him and dragging him into a pit. All those horrors ended when he helped his sister find a good man and got her out of the life of crime. He didn't know where she was anymore, but sometimes she thanked him in her dreams. Both sisters thanked him.

Later, he was sent to Siberia for stealing some official's car. Life got hard again. He was sorry that he did those horrible things to me. But he couldn't afford to show his weakness, because other criminals would judge him; it was a criminal code. But when there was a young girl sent to the camp, everything changed. He wanted to protect her like he did his sisters, but other criminals saw it as a weakness and wanted to kill him. But a good doctor took him in with that girl he was protecting. She was weak, but the doctor and other villagers helped her recover. The girl always asked who the man that saved her was. The doctor pointed at the man with tattoos on his chest. She wanted to be closer to him, even if he was without a leg and had had a horrible past.

At the moment, I understood the meaning of life. If someone like him could be loved, there could be a chance for me. But why should I be loved? Who had I saved?

Days went on and on, people were coming to the hospital and leaving. Many stories of broken people from many Baltic countries, Belarus, Ukraine, Poland, Russia, and other places -have come to the clinic. People started to build homes around the hospital. We built a secret church. There were a few people who were priests in their countries. They were prosecuted and followed by the communist regime. Their only sin was that they spread their Christian faith. Many things happened back then. The war and terror spread like wildfire. Stories were getting worse and worse. The war damaged many lives and people were getting desperate. Russians were having more and more casualties. Towns were burned, people starving and many other horrors performed by the German and even by the Soviet army. People could be shot in the streets just for losing their documents. Rape, torture and all other horrors were transmitted through the radio station that one of the engineers secretly built and hid in the cellar.

Many nations were participating in the war. Americans were battling in Japan and sending support to England. Russians were fighting in Stalingrad, one of the fiercest battles in World War II, where millions of people gave up their lives. One rifle was allocated to two soldiers because the resources were scarce and factories couldn't produce the required number of rifles and ammunition. People went into the fight with almost bare hands and empty stomachs. Siberia wasn't much different; a lump of bread was shared between 10 or more people. We had to survive, there was no other choice. The ones who were selfish and didn't share were made outcasts and after some time, they understood their fault and were given a small portion of food to survive. But some of them who were too selfish and ungrateful for the small portion of food didn't survive.

We tried to grow some food ourselves. Some people brought potatoes to Siberia. They were real lifesavers. They hid the potatoes inside their coats and pockets of their inside clothes. We planted the potatoes in spring and we reaped our harvest in the autumn. The most important thing was that if you put horses, pigs, cows dung in the ground when planting the potatoes, you would reap ten times the harvest. This was because minerals in the poo acted like fertilizer and helped the potatoes to grow. Nothing is more important than food and water except human life. You can survive without many things in life. But you will always need food and water.

Sometimes people forget what life is really about, they start chasing things, like luxury, money, valuables and fake ideals. They start following people who promise them success. But those successful people are more broken then everybody else because success makes them blind to people's problems. Why do we become so distant from each other? Why do we value money over someone close to us? Why don't we see our parents' dedication, until it's too late? Why do we ever try to reach something too big, when we already have everything? Our thirsts for bigger, stronger, faster will only have us smashing into the first tree on the road.

I used to look at the lake and relax. It made me calm. Somehow, everything made sense. You look into the water, see how it flows; it doesn't feel anger or need for revenge, it just goes through ground, calm and relaxed and flowing water makes you calm. Somehow, the water makes us think and relaxes the body. People must stay humble about the power of water. Water can bear life, water can be cold as ice, it can become a cloud, it can rain on you, you can dance in the rain or you can cry in the rain, it's your choice. If you're not careful, water can kill you. Life is full of choices; most of them are clear, but some are hidden behind the clouds that protect us. We are destined for greatness, but we must learn from our past and think about the future and, most importantly, be in the present. Enjoy the small things in life. There are very few magical moments in our life and sometimes we forget how fragile we are. Those moments are so close that we rush too much in life without seeing them. Parents and grandparents are the most important people you should take care of. Your grandparents and parents will share their infinite wisdom with you. And wisdom is one of the most important things to have. In my little town, there were people who think like zombies, they have their small portion of happiness in the bottle or other temporary joys, but they don't see other people. They don't see the miracles in the world. When Jews walked in the desert and God gave them holy manna, they all considered it a miracle. Sometimes, there are miracles all around us. God always sent gifts to us from heaven. The biggest gifts are children. Nothing is more precious and nothing is more demanding.

My leg was getting better. I talked with the person who did those horrible things to me and he didn't seem so horrible anymore. He was more pleasant, the woman who he saved was taking care of him. I tried to help them by chopping some wood for their little home because they didn't have lots of hands and it seemed I could help. The most important thing isn't vengeance or hatred, its forgiveness, and love. By helping others, we help ourselves. And nothing is truer than that. Even if he was my enemy, I tried my best, because it was a choice I made. It was a troubled time and I had to help them because I could. Most of the time, the ones who were hurt help those who are suffering. The warmth comes from within and we must accept people for who they are. Jesus taught that we must love our enemies. It's the hardest love of all, but I remembered many stories of people who came here to Siberia. They were sent from all parts of the Soviet Union. Some people were sent here because they fell in love with the wrong person, some had spoken something about politics, some were hiding their food from the government, some were generals who cherished their soldiers, some of them were priests, teachers, doctors, and even communist party members, some of them were children or elderly people and some of them were just at the wrong place at the wrong time. This place was horrible, but somehow joining our efforts made us work together and help each other. The doctor helped me, so I helped others; I kept my word no matter what. I had to because it was the most important thing to do. Helping others is a choice, it's a choice that is written in the bible or in someone's heart. I tried my best to follow my heart and be the best person I could be. I helped others to plant food to teach them the stories of life. I tried to be an inspiration to others, to help one another, to live a holy life. Sometimes, only prayers kept many people going through life at those times.

My leg hurt, but it didn't matter, I tried to forget my problems because there were people with much bigger problems than my leg. We gathered freezing people from the woods; they looked terrible. We gave them hot water and tea. Sometimes, we had to amputate fingers, a leg or a hand. It wasn't easy, but we continued on.

The years went on and on, we planted vegetables in spring and gathered the harvest in autumn. There were a few joys after all. We had a secret church in the basement, and we prayed for every new soul that joined our small group. Somehow, the town began to grow, more and more people were coming in. We built new houses, gathered and chopped firewood. The small little Siberian place started developing into a small country town. I told stories about my country, many people never heard about such a beautiful country. They listened to me like I was telling a fairytale to a group of children. Many people that gathered here didn't have such a beautiful childhood like mine. They were poor, broken and lost people. Their own friends or family members betrayed them and gave them up to Soviet soldiers. Adolf Hitler was pure evil. 6 million Jews were starved to death, put into gas chambers, executed in mass graves and killed by people who felt no remorse and no feelings for the pain of others. Handicapped, the sick, children, the elderly; no one was an exception for the Nazis. Stalin was not a Good Samaritan either. He had an Iron Fist, not only for people from other countries but to his own people as well. People told stories of the horrible inhumane conditions they were kept in and tortured. The criminal rage was rampaging over Europe like a disease, the two superpowers Nazi Germany and the Soviet Union were at each other throats and everyone else was just collateral damage.

NEW CHAPTER

I didn't know what kept us all going. I guess we followed our hearts and just carried on through the tough times. Alone we were weaker, but when we were united and helped each other by sharing a potato or piece of bread, we became stronger, united under one flag. And that flag was life. We cherished each other even through the toughest times, because hard times reveal people, only then can you see the true color of a person. The doctor was the best of us; he worked day and night to help the sick, wounded and desperate. I tried to help him as best I can, my leg was getting better but somehow I still felt pain and couldn't be as useful as I wanted. I dreamt about that girl in the fields almost every night. She was my strength to carry on.

Once, I helped an old lady in our small village. She was somehow different from all the people I met before. She had a good heart and was very important to all the people in the village. She was very wise and good-hearted. She had no kids, but she adopted a few children and helped them to survive the harsh times we were in. Somehow she understood me; she looked right through people because she was smart and could understand our hopes and dreams. I told her about my dreams and when she listened, she was a little upset.

"You're a good person and I wanted you to stay with us for longer. But your future isn't among us. You love your country too much to live somewhere else. One day you will leave us, but until that day you should help as many people as you can, because one day the war will be over, but there will always be people you can help. No matter what time we will be living in and no matter where God takes us. You should always remember that helping others is the best gift that God has given us."

I always remember her words. She was the smartest person I have ever met. All my life, I have remembered her advice. She smiled all the time and was cheerful even in the hardest times. Something was bright about her; she had a good heart and knew more than everybody else. Such people were much respected at our times because wise people helped survive the harsh times we were in. Everybody could hear the stories told by other people, they all were interested in the outcome of the war because one person had made a radio set in secret. We all listened to the radio, but many people were scared because the radio also transmitted propaganda. We couldn't know what was true and what was false for certain. There was always false information. With data nowadays, you can check what is false and what is true, a luxury we didn't have back in our days.

The Second World War ended on 2 September 1945 when Nazi Germany agreed on total capitulation. There were cheers and joy on all radio stations. But sadly, the war didn't end for many people in my country, the people were still sent to work camps for relocation. Most of them were priests, teachers, doctors, professors, educated and wealthy people. The people who were sent were the ones who could stand against the communist political party. Sometimes, they even sent children and elderly people. The people in the world celebrated the victory against Nazi Germany, but my country still struggled against the oppressive communist regime. All over the world people cheered and rejoiced, but we were under the foot of the communist party. Everything around the world had changed; the cities were getting rebuilt from the rubble. The people were joyful and happy, but the trains with political prisoners were still coming in.

We tried to work as hard as we could; we helped one another and the ones who were weaker. We used to grow food together and share it among all the people. We were in pain but we had to endure. We couldn't live like animals, because animals wouldn't survive in a gulag. There was one person named Troika. He wasn't a good man; he stole food from others, started beating the ones who were weaker, almost raped a woman in the village, and everyone called him a wolf. The wolf didn't survive long. Many people were fed up with him and hanged him on a tree in the nearest forest. Sometimes, when food was scarce we used to gather in the nearest barn and secretly shared what we had, some people had nothing so we gave them a little from ourselves so that more people could survive.

We buried Troika, even with the horrible things he did and the pain he caused for so many people. Troika was a real animal, even the cruel thieves in law despised him. But we had a tradition of burying dead people; to bury the dead is considered one of the most important Lithuanian traditions. We also look after the graves of our passed relatives. It is very important for Lithuanians to remember the ones who have gone and remember them in prayer. I don't remember how many people we buried; every time the winter came, more and more people were getting new diseases and more and more people were sent to the graveyard. The doctor tried his best, but there were simply too many people for all of us to handle and too little medicine to help everyone that needed help. Sometimes, we would amputate a whole hand or whole fingers because people working in the gulags were physically and morally abused by the Soviet guards. Our small village wasn't stagnant either. We were rearing a number of cows and chickens. We learned how to make candles from animal fat. We even had a horse from a nearby farm so we could plow the land.

Soldiers still treated us like animals, but we knew that we had to go on because if we didn't, the next winter could be our last. We secretly stole small wood sticks from the forest, even though we weren't allowed to because the forest was government property and we could have been shot for stealing. Many people couldn't gather firewood so we all helped everyone as best as we could.

The scariest time of all was in the winter. Resources were scarce and we didn't knew what to expect from forest wolves who were getting more and more aggressive, because they were used to the taste of human flesh during the war. We bashed their heads with wooden sticks, but sometimes they came back for chickens and other domestic animals. In winter, we used to gather in the big barn we built for the hay and discuss what actions to take, how to distribute the food and how to prepare better for the next winter. The old lady was considered the wisest and her words and knowledge were considered the most important. The doctor was also much respected and considered one of the most important people in the community. People were secretly sent to nearby villages to exchange the medicine needed for sick people. Many of us had to come through hell, just to survive; we had to ration the food in winter. Sometimes, we ate only one potato in a day, just to survive those horrible times.

I had problems with pain, my leg hurt almost every winter, because of a lack of vitamins and calcium. The only calcium we could get those days was from the milk and we gave all the milk to children and elderly people because they needed it more. The most horrible loss was the death of a cow because cows gave us offspring and always provided milk. Of course, we could eat the flesh of a cow, but a bucket of milk was more precious than a dead cow. Milk was the most important product back in those days and nothing could replace it.

We worked hard, perhaps even extremely hard. The fields were vast and very demanding. We had to plow the ground after the rain because it was rock solid and with lots of clay in it. We had to plant lots of potatoes because there were lots of mouths to feed and we all wanted to survive the next winter. We protected our animals as best as we could because they gave us milk, eggs, meat and natural fertilizer that made our harvest ten times bigger. We grew pigs and they made a hell of a lot of the fertilizer, but fresh meat and bacon always tasted the best in the winter. We smoked the meat and made it last for long periods of time.

Life was hard and new patients kept coming in. At times when things seemed to be getting better, when the harvest was beginning to grow and we thought we could sustain the number of people in the village, more victims of the Soviet regime were joining our community and we had to start the carousel all over again, because we had to raise our food production to sustain the numbers of our new fellows in common despair. Those people were lost, cold, and hungry and we just couldn't leave them like that. Because for every new member of our community, we had a new pair of hands, a new pair of feet, a new head, full of wisdom and a new mind, full of courage. In this community, we found out that everyone is important and everyone is needed; the smallest and the biggest, the strongest and the weakest, the tallest and the shortest. Everyone mattered. We had a few Asian people, lots of Russians, someone from Uzbekistan; he was a short man, but with a big heart, a Muslim and a few criminals. But even the criminals understood our goal to survive, we were all in the same boat and everyone had to paddle synchronically. If we didn't, we simply wouldn't survive till the next winter.

The most important thing was to care for the children. We knew that they wouldn't survive without us adults. Children were our hope. They were the most important to us because we felt that they one day could have a better life than we did and live in a better world that we had. We put all our hopes and dreams into them. We taught them everything about life and tried to teach them to care for each other and to create a better world than we live in now and care for other people; the elderly, weaker ones, the ones who were broken inside and outside. Important things are the simplest of them all. Most importantly, you should have water and bread on your table, you have to have a roof over your head and you should have your loving family. We all were a family and that was the most important thing we had in our lives. We were all broken, but we stood together and didn't hate the government that treated us badly; we didn't have time for that. We had our small problems, like crops, potatoes, taking water to the cows, feeding the pigs. Somehow, everything else wasn't that important, we had to worry about the food on the table, not about Stalin's architectural plans in Moscow or Saint Petersburg. We tried to teach our kids to be good people, not to be rich. We didn't have money there. It was useless. We had to exchange goods and services. Nobody would trade a cow for paper. That was stupid. Food was scarce and goods were even scarcer. Clothes were a real luxury item because we didn't have lots of fabric to make them. We had to make clothes for the children from our own clothes; we exchanged scissors, threads, and needles with other villages. Most importantly, if we had newborn children, we had to think up a way to keep them safe and warm, because many newborns could die in such horrible conditions and we kept the best food and cow milk for the younglings. I never knew how much suffering people could withstand until I got to Siberia. There, I lived in the most horrible conditions possible with the best people I ever met in my life. Sometimes, I think withstanding these conditions made me a cold person. It made me more distant from people, but at the same time, I could feel the pain of others and could understand how they feel, even just by looking at them. This made me selfless and more compassionate to others. I could understand what they were going through and I could help them as much as I could. Being selfish and self-centered is the biggest sin anyone could commit because selfishness will only bring people to disaster and can even crumble the strongest communities or even countries. We are all dependent on each other one way or another and if we try to deny our social duties we will fall and crumble even at the smallest of things. We have to live in peace with each other and in peace and harmony with Mother Nature because it gives us the most important things we have. If we deny that fact in the future, we will have so many problems that not even the Holy Spirit can help us.

Some people deny the importance of life itself, they deny this in favor of money and capital growth, but you can't eat money, you can't use the money for clothing and you can't replace love with money. Love for one another is the most important thing that no one can take away from you. Mother Theresa said:

The hunger for love is much more difficult to remove than the hunger for bread.

If people knew how their grandparents lived, they would cry in tears and thank God for the life they have. Working their whole life in the empty fields, full of sweat. Pain in the arms and legs was a common feeling for many of your elders, but their sweat was important because it put food on the table and they valued every crumb of bread they had. Now, people throw away food for no reason and don't value what they have. Everything is made for them in the factories and sold in the supermarkets. People got so distant from the production of food that some people think that bread and meat grow in the supermarket. They have no idea how the food is made and how much sweat people used to put in just to have food on their table. Food is sacred; no one should throw away food and disrespect it. In our country, if people threw away food after a few weeks the family would face some kind of tragedy and most of the time it would be a horrible one, because food, in our culture, is sacred.

Many people think of wealth and happiness, but we didn't have that luxury; we had to work day and night just to survive. Food was scarce and commodities like medicine, clothes, lamps, salt, and other important items were nowhere to be found, we had to rely only on ourselves to make some goods or face the hard conditions of wintertime. Wood was really important because it provided the heat to our small cabins and without heat, we would surely be lost in winter. Food was scarce; we surely couldn't feed everyone the way we wanted. We gave the best pieces of food to children and the elderly and everything else we distributed among ourselves. You have to understand that taking care of the weaker part of society is the most important goal that anyone could have. Especially the children who can't take care of themselves; they always need our care and attention. It's in the human nature to help the weaker part of the community and society.

Our little village was growing day by day; we couldn't understand why the Soviet government sent so many people to gulags. The war was over, why it was needed to get rid of the people who were just asking some different questions and fought for their rights was a mystery. We even had war generals and members of the communist party sent to us. It looked like everyone who didn't smile right was sent to Siberia.

The generals were really useful, they went through the war and they knew what was at stake, because hunger, low goods, and despair were a part of their life not so long ago. Generals worked the hardest and helped us ration food better. The communist party politician was not so helpful; in fact, he was the opposite. His washed-up brain made everyone angry, but we still helped him survive because we needed a pair of hands.

Days went by and by. I was about 20 years old when I was sent to Siberia; the days of my youth were spent in that place. Cold, miserable and broken, we were all changed, whether young or old, we all faced the most horrible trials in our life in Siberia. Was it the hunger, the scarcity of everything or the pain in the people's faces? Everything was darker; we all knew that our life might end in that place. Some of the people got used to our place of exile so much that they forgot their homes, but I didn't. I dreamt of that girl in my dreams for as long as I could remember. Somehow, I knew that place in my dreams; I knew that it was my country. But those were only dreams and every time I woke up, I knew that I might never see my country again. The people kept coming in, but no one was getting out. If we tried, the soldiers and KGB officers would quickly put us in the gulags again or even shoot on sight. Everybody knew that; we had no papers, so we were exiles in a country that didn't want us.

I learned Russian pretty fast because most of the people in the village were Russians. They had become victims of their own government. It was a tragedy for all of them; they had been betrayed by their own. Some of them were even in positions of power, but a younger and more flexible person was put in their place. Some of them were peasants who were hiding their own planted food from the government. Some people were sent to the gulag because they fell in love with the wrong person. Some had been reading the wrong books or listened to the wrong radio stations. Many people were sent to Siberia just because they were priests or faithful people and religion was considered a crime in the Soviet Union. Some of the people were here because they didn't want to go to war for the Soviet Union or despised the policy or ideology of the government. Or like that 7-year old boy who was just pasting pamphlets on the street. That was the price the people paid for the glory of the Soviet Union and nothing else was more important to the government than protecting themselves from the 7-year old boy who was just sticking pieces of paper in the streets. I couldn't understand that, even when I tried. How the mighty Soviet Union could be threatened by a young seven-year-old helpless child. If the Soviet Union was so powerful and strong and mighty, how could one small child cripple one of the mightiest empires in human history? I understood one thing then. Maybe that empire isn't that strong anyway and could break one day or another.

NEW CHAPTER

We worked hard day after day just to survive because nothing really mattered more than a piece of bread or a potato. You have to remember that after the war, the resources were scarce and we had to exchange with other villages just to make ends meet. Sometimes they gave us food, sometimes we shared our own. We had our little economy going and you can say we were the first businessmen in the Soviet Union. We needed not only food but goods. Goods were hard to get because they were at low supply. The whole world was just recovering from the war; nobody cared about some prisoner villages in Siberia. All the best products from factories were sent to Moscow and Saint Petersburg and we were left on our own. Nobody cared about villages in the outskirts of the great Siberian forests. We were the low of the lowest of the Soviet society and nobody cared about the lowest and long-forgotten people. We were like the untouchables in India. There were lots of places like ours all over the Soviet empire. We were just a small part of a big picture that comprised of more than four million people imprisoned in such camps, many of them having much worse conditions than ours. Some war factories now became factories of goods. They made milk bottles, clothes, bed sheets, furniture, and bread. The most important were the factories of steel, oil, gas and other goods that could be exported. Also, the cities had to be rebuilt so the factories that made construction materials like bricks, cement, and concrete were also essential to the Soviet Regime. But the most important part of Soviet power was still the military complex and German scientists were in the highest demand by both sides; the Soviets and the West. They were of the highest value. Technology was always on the top of the game and it was the sweetest pie of them all. This was the beginning of the Cold War - the biggest competition in the world between the Soviet Union and the West. The West built the atomic bomb. The Soviets stole the secrets and built theirs. The Soviets were first to send a satellite, the Sputnik to outer space; they sent the first animals and the first man to space and they were also the ones who sent a man to walk in space. But the Americans were the first ones to land on the Moon and return back safely.

From all the human achievements in history, I think the most valuable ones are the ones that taught us to make food in the quantities that we required. Life without food is none existent. We can travel to space, achieve speeds faster than sound, and look beyond our solar system. But if we can't make food for ourselves, it won't matter, because, without food and water, there is no life. If we become capable of surviving without food, then we wouldn't be human anymore; we would be something else, something darker and crueler and that is a future I would never want to face. Food is life and life is food. That it's how it's meant to be. Maybe in the afterlife, when we leave our bodies and don't require our physical body to function, we would be able to survive without food. But in this life and in this world, food is essential.

How many people tried to enslave others against their will? How many of them perished and how many will perish after them? It's an endless cycle and if we don't put an end to it, we will perish. People have tried to enslave others since the beginning of time. They used others for their needs, to build their roads, to build their monuments, to build their castles and walls, to fight for them in their armies and for what? For scraps from their table. What those people did will echo in the songs of thousands and millions of the wounded, paralyzed, betrayed, left behind and disregarded. Their songs will reach the skies and echo in the darkness. Everything will be remembered and nobody will be discouraged and ashamed, because the cries of the many will reach the ears of the few who will have the power to listen and determine their fate.

You have to push forward, no matter what. You just have to go on. You can't give up for any reason, just follow your dream and be persistent. To be persistent, even in the smallest things, is the most important thing ever. If you don't give up, you will have big opportunities in your life, sometimes the opportunities present in the times of your struggles. When you are struggling, just continue because if you continue to work on your dream and be persistent you will surely reach your goal. Even the hardest of goals can be achieved by you if you never ever, ever give up. You have to go on, even in the hardest of times because other people rely on you, you are responsible not only for yourself but for others. Perhaps you have responsibilities for your family, for your community, for your city or for your country. You are not alone, there is always someone cheering for you even if you don't know it.

Our days in the Gulag were hard as hell, we all came back from the fields tired and hungry, our food supply was low, but our will was strong. We had to work just to survive and nothing else was more important. We had others who couldn't work or were sick or were weaker than us and we had to care for them. If we didn't do our part, many people would die. The exchange of goods with other villages was a critical skill to our survival and for these tasks, we sent our best and strongest to negotiate and exchange the things we needed. Sometimes, they would come back with a deal that wasn't in our favor, but we needed to make sacrifices because we knew that there was a bigger picture and other villages had problems like ours. Sometimes the deal was bad, sometimes it was really good because other villages had a bigger harvest and wanted to share their good fortune with us. We knew we had to work as an intelligent economical unit because we simply had no choice, we had to survive. You could say we learned the rules of international trade really quickly because when resources are low, all your other abilities strengthen in a very short time. You use intelligence, wisdom, negotiation, and cleverness to obtain your goals and an empty stomach is the biggest motivator you can get. But other villages were also clever; they negotiated two pairs of warm clothes for four big bags of potatoes. That was a huge win for them because their food supply was really low and we had a significant amount of potato harvest that year.

If you think you have problems, tell it to our grandparents, they would really like to hear them because their problems were at least 100 times bigger than yours. They lived through the Second World War, they worked their asses off, survived multiple financial crises, and went through so many problems that are unimaginable in your present day. You can't even imagine what comforts you have now. Grandparents have the most wisdom you would ever find. Their knowledge is endless and their wisdom is limitless. After all, they came through all the struggles you are experiencing right now, know how hard it is for you and how much you are struggling with your problems. And if you listen to your grandparents, they just might provide a solution for the trouble you are going through right now.

We all have our problems and most problems are solvable. But you can never solve one problem; the problem of death. When somebody dies, you can never get them back, so spend time with your grandparents while you still can, because one day they will be gone and you will be very sad that you didn't spend more time with them. The problem with death is that it is inevitable; we all will have to die one day. This is how it goes. But even the law of physics tells us that there is some form of afterlife. The law of conversion of energy says that energy is never created nor destroyed, but changes form. That means that the energy we are created from has to come from something and has to transform into something after we die.

Many people live life like they are eternal, they work from day to day never thinking and asking themselves if their work is meaningful or what they will accomplish in life besides working long hours and living from paycheck to paycheck. The people who think about the meaning of life and the things that matter the most get out of this circle that we get into from when we are children and have to go to school every single day. I understand that you have to learn, the skill to learn is the most important skill you will ever have in life, but what's next? What are your goals? What do you want to achieve in life? If your goal in life is to buy a new Lamborghini or a Bentley when you are 50 then you are probably good, having such a life. But is that all? Your world has to be expanded every single day; your mind has to be open to new ideas. For spiritual ideas, your health and fitness mentality, economic prosperity, serving others, love, more compassion, books and studies, personal growth, teaching others, helping others in need, learning more than you have ever dreamt of, travel, wonderful food, new experiences, meeting spiritual and other mentors, learning from the best, bearing children and of course living are great examples. By living, I mean not existing like a robot, but having a real meaningful life. You have to choose, nobody can do it for you.

After all, who am I to tell you that, I'm just a person sitting in Siberia, with a bunch of political criminals and outcasts? We only had a few potato bags in our secret stash and a few loafs of bread hidden somewhere around the village. It's your choice, my friend, your decision to make, not mine, I know the choices I will make, the decisions I have to take, and the sacrifices I have to come through. After all, you are reading this book, not me. Do you probably want to find out what is next? I will tell you. But now I need sleep, my bones hurt from carrying heavy bags of potatoes from one corner of the village to another. Let me sleep a little and tomorrow I will tell what comes next.

NEW CHAPTER

I woke up early in the morning and could still feel the pain in my back. I tried to calm down. That day, soldiers came to the village, they took some food and other things from us. We were glad we had been preparing for a day like this because we had secret stashes everywhere and yesterday we moved our main potato stash to another location. It was deep in the woods and hidden from the eyes of the soldiers. The soldiers were afraid of the woods because wolves and other animals used to attack other villages from time to time. Animal hunger for human flesh was a big danger for any man alive. But we feared hunger more than some pack of wolfs. Do you think we couldn't fight the wolves? You are wrong. We brought axes and faced a wolf with an ax. It's not so dangerous. The most important thing was to ensure you didn't get an infection from a bite.

Soviet soldiers were cruel. They took everything they could find and gave nothing back. In Siberia, there is only one law; survive at all costs. Life is hard there. We had our small community and that community protected us; if we were alone, one by one, we would be long gone by now. We were like wolves. Individually, we were weak but united, we were stronger than ever. We prepared wood together, planted and gathered harvest together, gathered in the secret meetings to discuss our affairs, had our own trials and the people who misbehaved were banished from our village because we had no luxury of time to deal with people who didn't understand our basic values and belief system. Also, we didn't have the ability to eat three meals a day if somebody wanted it. Most of all, we didn't have the will to take care of people who wanted to harm others or make other damage to the community. Most of us understood the position we were in and followed the rules we had. But sometimes we had to make a tough choice to exclude someone, just because there was no other way.

We made tough choices, but we had to because there were other people that counted on us. For these people to survive, we needed to make the rations better, distribute and save food for the rainy day and work our hardest to gather the harvest. The relations with other villages were essential; other villages made bread, we produced potatoes. Other villages had more tools, and we had more clothes. The exchange of items was made by the strongest and wisest people in our village. They knew what we needed and had to bargain their best. Many of the people who were in charge knew what was at stake and that we had low resources, so every lump of bread and every bucket of potatoes mattered. I won't even talk about meat, eggs, and milk. They were the products of luxury, especially meat. Fresh meat was considered gold and every chicken, pig, and cow was considered the highest value resource. Now, you can choose a huge variety of foods and drinks; in our time it would be considered heaven here in Siberia. None of us could ever even dream of things, goods and opportunities you have now. You live in a life of prosperity and growth; you remember times like ours only in horror stories and the history channel. What could you say to a child who hadn't eaten for a few days straight? What could you say to a person who lost five of his fingers to frostbite, to a mother who lost all of her five children to war, to a father who can't even give his daughter a lump of bread? And most of all what can you say to millions of people tortured and put to gas chambers by Nazi SS soldiers.

Many people live from day to day and don't even understand what fortune they have. They have almost all the luxuries of life and still think they are entitled to something. They want to change their life somehow but don't know that they already have everything. They have a beautiful family, but they still cheat on their wife, a big house, but they want a mansion, a new car, but they want a Lamborghini. Life is a circle of things we want. We think that we will be happy if we get this or that, but in reality, when chasing something else we lose what is most important. We lose the things we have; your grandma and your grandpa will die one day, so spent time with them. Your parents will die too so cherish them. Your girlfriend or your wife is the only one who loves you so cherish them. Your kids will go out and start their own families, so spend time with them. You have to know that all the things in life are temporary. Even you aren't immortal, so remember that everything matters and the small things you do for your family members are very important. You have to know that only you can change yourself and be grateful for what you have.

I took many things for granted in my day, but when I was in Siberia I knew that my life was beautiful and I had a wonderful childhood, my parents were the best people I could ever find and I loved them from the bottom of my heart. I knew that no one would love me more than my parents did and somehow, from time to time, I felt lonely in the Siberian village.

I still had dreams about that girl who made my mind think of better days when this all was over and I would return back to Lithuania. But those were only dreams, and only those dreams were keeping me sane in the situation I was in. Cold, hunger and pain were constant in my life. They were the only real currency I had in my pocket and my days flew by like months. We had so much work and so much to do that we couldn't even think about rest. Our world was small and poor. We were full of anger and pain, but we carried on; we had to because we needed to survive and we needed each other.

Sometimes, the days were so bad that we had only one potato in a day because we had such scarce resources, we could only feed the people with what we had. Thank God the water supply was almost endless. The things we did would seem crazy in your time. We tried to feed people with water. When people felt very hungry and we had close to nothing, sometimes we would suggest they had a cup of water. It is very dangerous and could lead to serious sicknesses, but on some days, it looked like the only choice we had. There were days we had only a potato for a whole day. For the morning and evening meals, we would give people a cup of water if they were hungry. You have to remember it's very dangerous for your health and I don't recommend doing it.

I was walking down the road with one man when I heard screams in one of the houses. We ran near the house and found a man was trying to rape a woman. We pulled him off the woman, punched him in the head repeatedly and dragged him to a local farmhouse. The elders soon knew about the incident. All the people gathered to the trail. We all knew the consequences of such behavior. He tried to beg us and say he would never do it again, but the decision was already made and he was excluded from our community. He had to leave as soon as possible. He cried his heart out, but the decision of the elders was final. We had no other choice. He packed all of his belongings. We gave him some food for the road and he left us. None of us heard of him since. Our rules were strict and we had to follow them. If we didn't have rules, we would be nothing more than animals and nothing is worse than losing your humanity.

Many days went by, our resources started to grow gradually. The harvest this year was extremely rich and we could even help other villages a little more. Somehow, the new arrivals seemed to dwindle. We wondered what had happened. People wondered if Stalin's fist had become weaker. It turned out it didn't. People were just sent into deeper parts of Siberia where conditions were even harsher. There was a new major sent to monitor the wood production in the gulag. He was different, younger and viler than the one before. He hated our small village and despised our way of life, but he couldn't do anything, because his only concern was the wood production sent to the factories in the Soviet Union. We later found out that he was sent here as a punishment. He seduced one of the daughters of a high-standing KGB officer. If he wasn't the son of an influential communist party member, he probably would be sent here with us or executed at some secret criminal prison.

The major was a really cruel person; he treated the people of gulag with disrespect. He would burn down our village if he could, but his authority among soldiers was weak. He was considered a weak-minded young major who was sent here to do his sentence. The only concern of the young major was the women of the gulag. He would bring in the women he liked to his cabin and he would do anything he wanted with them. He was a cruel and vile person. He treated others like meat; he would beat the prisoners for no reason and treated the women extremely poorly. Every person in the gulag hated him. He was such an evil person that even the scum of the gulag didn't want to do anything with him.

We helped the people we could and the caretaker of the gulag was young and inexperienced and that made our work a little easier. We were smarter. Much smarter than him and with our wisdom, we tricked him many times. He would visit our village, but he considered us outcasts, so it was easy to hide our stash or our progress. You could say he was young, stupid, very naïve and that made our lives easier. We would hide our girls and women in the woods when he conducted his visits and kept only ugly and old women for him to look at. He always despised us and told our men that we had the ugliest women he had ever seen in our village, when in fact, most of the women were in hiding. He had another weakness: cards and gambling. He would always owe his soldiers some favor that he lost while gambling. He owed almost every soldier some money and that made him even a bigger mockery in the gulag. He had small eyes and wore glasses. The Major also had a big nose and a big forehead, which made him look like a big Neanderthal with glasses. Some people thought he was stupid because he was born with a birth defect. And when he heard that, he drank a whole week and beat up every man and woman who got in his way. He became crazy; his eyes would almost pop up when talking to someone. He would scream and shout at everybody and later cry in the corner. Most of the time, he spent with the bottle and quoting the Soviet doctrine and principles of Lenin and Karl Marx. Everybody lost hope in him, but one person didn't. She was a young and sweet political prisoner who just wanted to help him. She started to take care of him and it looked like he was coming back to his senses. She believed in him somehow. Everybody wondered how that girl could take his expressions of rage, but somehow she was stubborn. That crazy man started walking through the gulag with her. The Major started to respect her and even listened to her advice. Things around the gulag even seemed to be getting better. The governor of the gulag started caring about the people a little. That was strange to all of us, how a man could change so fast. His drinking and gambling habits were dropped. That girl changed him. It was strange for all of us in the village because it seemed like someone like him could never change. He even brought food to our village sometimes; it was really strange to see him in the position of a caregiver. We got used to being treated like animals and when someone who was more of a pig and less of a person started to treat us nice, we considered it to be a big step forward into the future. But we still were cautious; somehow we knew that this wasn't going to last forever.

Things started to get better. Major bought a beautiful dress for his wonderful new girlfriend and even built some new toilets for the prisoners in the gulag. Our harvest was also pretty good. Everything seemed to be heading for the better. We started to live better; sometimes the Major himself would bring food to our village. His new girlfriend accompanied him all the time and seemed to become more beautiful and beautiful every day. We were all mesmerized; how can one person change such a monster so quickly? It was amazing to see him change so fast. We didn't know what to expect from him. Some days he would even bring some clothes for our people; it was like looking in a crooked mirror. The gulag governor became soft and gentle. The girl was always with him and giving him advice about everything, it seemed like they were never apart, even for a second.

How can anyone change so much? We all wondered if the girl put a spell on him or something. In a few months, he became a whole different person. The gulag was having the best days in its history. The soldiers didn't torture or beat the prisoners; the production of lumber was growing rapidly. People worked their hearts out because they knew that they would get food on the gulag table. We were also in great shape, we had a wonderful harvest and the trade relationship between the villages was at its peak. Everything was going just great. People in the gulag even seemed happy. We didn't have to drag the bodies of beaten-up prisoners to our clinic. Everything was changing for the better. The major's girlfriend even organized a monthly celebration for prisoners. Once in a month, people danced while soldiers clapped in the rhythm. She always danced with the major and nobody else. She was truly in love with him and it was obvious, even to a blind person. There was something in that girl; a warm spirit and a pure heart. Something that was so rare and unique that everybody who was looking at her could see. She was really beautiful, her eyes were brown and her long hair fitted her thin body just perfectly. Her slim and elegant figure would look beautiful in any man's hug. She wasn't tall; the right opposite, she was pretty short. But she had a figure that would impress any man who would look at her. It seemed that she would shiver every time the major kissed her. She was innocent as the first blossoming flowers in spring. She had everything that any man could ever desire or even dream of desiring. She was sweet and well-mannered, elegant and pretty. She was pure in her heart and soft in her character.

The days went on and we filled all of our stashes with potatoes. We had an excellent year, even other villages were jealous of our accomplishments. People were happy; the faces of some people were filled with smiles. Some of the people even started telling jokes. Those were the best times of our lives; nothing was better than those days. Even the iron fist of Stalin seemed gentler than before. People were happy, we even had Friday meetings to relax, talk, sing, and dance. The world was changing for us. We had our best time then, a couple even secretly married. We were full of joy in our minds and hearts. Somehow, everything seemed to be going our way and we were happy like never before. We even made bigger rations for the people of the village, but we were cautious, our inner voices told us that everything could change and the big bad major could return to his former self. After all, the wisdom of our elders stated that people don't change. But our situation showed differently; major wasn't changing by days, he was changing by minutes. We all respected the woman who had the ability to have such an effect on that person. She was the most respected person in the gulag. Everyone greeted her and gave her the biggest of smiles. Somehow that single person changed the lives of everyone in one of the most horrible places in the Soviet Union. We were all feeling the glory of God through her. She was the symbol of the best that this world could give.

Our days went on and on and the major made our lives better. Somehow his heart opened and our lives mattered. From being just the meat in the horrible Soviet machine, we finally could feel like actual people. Nothing inspired us more than the little girl from Poland, who was so bright and selfless that even angels sang when she walked through the street. Her smile made people's hearts feel full and joyful. Sometimes, we thought she was an angel who was sent from heaven to help us. She was so full of love and compassion that we thought to be impossible to achieve. Many of us greeted her with smiles and most of the time she greeted us back. Everything around the gulag was blossoming. We thought it was just a dream and that it couldn't be happening to us, but it did. Sometimes soldiers even carried the water for the sick people in the village. We were amazed that this was happening to us. The world was changing in front of our eyes and we just couldn't believe it. We were right not to believe it, but we only found that out later. The wisest people in the village told us not to rely on the change of a major so soon and that everything could change in an instant.

Days went on. The life in the gulag and our village flourished. We could say it was like a fairy tale come true. Food was not a luxury anymore, we felt more relaxed and safe. Our world was changing, from the anger in the people's faces, we could see more smiles. From despair, we could see more gratitude. The gulag was full of life like never before. We even held a dance party in one of the barns. Our life was getting better. We worked in the fields more joyfully. We told each other happier stories. Our world was beginning to have more color. We worked harder, but we were much happier. We had problems, but we overcame them. We made good relations with neighboring villages and we felt goodwill from the soldiers. Nothing could get us down; we were the ones on top, our will was strong and intentions were humble. We were the kings among all others and that was pretty clear. But there was a storm ahead of us and none of us could expect what would happen.

One day, the major somehow got drunk, and like in most stories, someone whispered something in his ear and after that, he did what he did.

Stories were told that soldiers found her stabbed to death and that there was blood all over majors' residence. The soldiers tried to bury her in secret, but we all knew what had happened. When the major got drunk and came home he shouted and yelled at her. She was scared and tried to escape, but he took a knife and everything else is just a simple story. After that everything changed, gulag prisoners were beaten worse than ever before. The major would bring women to his place, beat them and rape them. They would come back badly hurt and beaten. He would treat women horribly and he got away with it. All the soldiers in the gulag disrespected him and sometimes didn't obey his crazy orders. People wouldn't smile anymore. The women of our village cried day and night for the poor Polish girl who was stabbed for no reason. We all prayed for her because we knew how she was important to us and how much she had to suffer from the hands of that animal. Raping other women wasn't enough for him. He would bring prostitutes from a nearby town and drink with them until the morning. We didn't have it easy too. From being at the top, we were coming down very fast. The major had no concerns; he just needed more drinks and more women. But one day everything changed.

One day, the major came to our clinic. He had a rash of some sort on his body. The doctor examined him. It was clear. He had syphilis. There was no medicine for that disease at the time because every medical supply was low in Siberia. One soldier was sent to Moscow for a cure. We took the major to our clinic. He was suffering horribly, the rashes were all over his body and his temperature was rising very rapidly. He was having intense pain all over his body. We tried to give him some medicine for the pain, but the only cure he wanted was vodka. After a few days, he died; the soldier sent to Moscow came back too late. He died in horrible pain and everyone in our village said that he had earned it.

We all knew where the little Polish girl was buried in secret, so we dugout her body and reburied her in the local cemetery. It was a beautiful ceremony where everybody cried. Even some soldiers had come for the funeral. We will always remember her, no matter what. That person shined like the brightest star in the gulag and our village. We all remembered the wonderful thing she had done for all of us, some women cried the whole day and some men drank a whole bottle of moonshine vodka. We all knew that there would never be any one so precious in our lives like her again and we all stood still for a few minutes just to honor her. We didn't understand how anyone could hurt such an angel. Our hearts were bleeding out when we left her in the cemetery and we all knew that we would always remember her.

The days went by; we tried our best to survive. There was a new major sent to the gulag. He wasn't bad. He didn't interfere with our affairs and we didn't interfere with his, either. We felt at peace. Our days went on as usual. We had lots of work and didn't have time to look into everything that was happening in the gulag and nothing unexpected was happening. There were a few minor incidents, but nothing really horrible or misplaced. Everything returned to normal. We carried on with our lives and the new major carried on with his. He had his lumber orders from Moscow and we had our code of honor. Life became somewhat peaceful. We took our hard pill and continued on. We lived like nothing happened and tried to forget the horrible misfortune we had to face. All our anger was transformed into exceptional productivity in the fields. We had our biggest harvest ever and we all knew that our anger-transformed effort was getting us these amazing results. We had skin peeling from our hands, but it wasn't that important.

We all remembered the poor Polish girl and her bright smile that warmed our hearts. We all knew the price she had to pay for her warm soul and open mind. We all made a pact to never forget her and remember the sacrifice she had made.

NEW CHAPTER

Days went on and slowly our hearts healed. We took most of our time to harvest the potatoes and hide our stash of food from the soldiers. The more we worked, the more distant from the incident we felt. We tried to carry on as best we could. We made some beehives from lumber we got our hands on. We hid the beehives in the forest and I was appointed to be the keeper of the bees. Bees hated drunken people and I was one of the few who hated vodka. At first, it was hard; the bees stung me, but soon I learned how to take care of them. The next year we got our first honey. Everybody wanted to try the taste of honey and I was glad to provide our village with a valuable resource. The honey was put aside to be given to the sick people for its healing capability. In Lithuanian culture, there is only one creature that is considered equal to the human. It is the bee. Only this creature has so many songs and legends about it. It is the only creature worthy to have a place alongside humans, because of its work and dedication to its hive and his brothers.

Time past by and nothing was changing; our small group in the village was growing. We helped the people who were evicted from the gulag and those people helped us with knowledge and strength. We all tried our best to survive and help others to live through the madness and pain we all were suffering. We all had to do our part and no one was excluded from the group. Everyone had their part in the gathering, sorting and cleaning. My contribution was seen by the elders and I was considered of the highest value in the community. I helped not only in the fields but also at the medical center and people who could help other people were considered of the highest value. The elders wanted to marry me with somebody so I would contribute and stay in our community even if things changed. But I was having these dreams of that wonderful girl in those beautiful fields near the lake. When I told them about my dreams, they quit trying to marry me with somebody;

they knew I had a different future from theirs, a future destined only for me and nobody else.

We gathered enough potatoes to buy a cow and a bull and we made an exchange with the other villages. Our life really changed at that point; we had plenty of milk and a young calf every year. We exchanged a calf for some tools and food that we needed. The things were getting better and better; the fist of Stalin didn't seem as strong anymore. But we remembered our past and weren't certain that we could relax so soon. Our circle of friends got bigger. There were new villages like ours growing in the neighborhood. We taught them how to plant and harvest food, they gave us some portion of their harvest for our support and our grim past seemed more distant. The people felt better, but they were scared because the last time they felt better everything was torn to pieces and our lives shattered like glass. Our life became manageable; we trusted our people more and we relaxed little by little. The new major seemed not to care about our affairs and that made our life a whole lot better. After all, we were so used to being tormented and crushed that we were living in the same conditions of war as before. We thought that this life of struggle would never come to an end, but like many times before, we were wrong and we never expected that our salvation would come so soon and we all could choose a better life.

One day in our community we had a new member. She was a young political prisoner from some part of Asia. She was very beautiful and she worked hard. She quickly became very respected in our community. She wasn't strong, but with our help, we managed to build her and a few other people a house. She always smiled at me and seemed happy all the time. She was different; she had a very pure heart. Many men looked at her, but she only had her eyes on me. I was embarrassed because the only thing on my mind was my small village home in Lithuania and that girl in my dreams. The young Asian girl was very beautiful; she was short, but her eyes sparkled. She had the most beautiful smile I had ever seen. She tried to be closer to me and I felt her presence every time we went to work. She was strong even when she was so small. Something about her reminded us of the young Polish girl. All the men in the village tried to protect her. We all knew that she was important and tried to hide her when soldiers would come to the village. She had a pure heart and we all felt it. All of the men sworn to protect her and defend her from the problems she might face. She always tried to be closer to me, but I didn't want her to have any ideas when we were alone. I knew the price I would pay if I hurt her and I remembered my oath to the other men. After some time, the elders agreed that I should be her protector. They knew me pretty well and they hoped that in her arms, I would forget my country and stay among them to the end of my days. But every night in my dreams, I was running in those open fields that made me feel more alive like nothing before. Those dreams, that beautiful girl in Lithuania and those open fields mesmerized me.

With time, things got better and better. The new major turned out to be a warm-hearted person who survived the war and knew the value of people's lives. He seemed very at ease with the prisoners and even sent soldiers to help plant the fields and gather the crops and potatoes. He was a decent man and everyone in the villages spoke highly of him. He was older and knew how to behave with us and how to handle the difficult people in the gulag. He prohibited the beating of prisoners and punished those prisoners who would beat others. He quickly became one of the most respected people in the region. He even took us to a nearby city to purchase medicine for the sick people and he paid for it from his salary. After that act of kindness, every man in the village and every prisoner would shake his hand and thank him for his warm heart and bright soul. He was a good man, he talked about his wife and two children and that he would want to visit them more often but he had orders to stay in this gulag for a few years. Everybody was happy and wanted him to stay longer because his warm heart and good intentions were felt among every prisoner and villager who had the highest level of respect for him. You can see the beauty of a person, but you can't see the wisdom right away. People usually welcome people for their looks but value them for their wisdom. Looks are temporary, but wisdom is endless. The biggest mistake people make is that they value people only for their social status rather than value them for a person she or he is. Sometimes, a rather poor person is much wealthier in the heart than the rich and influential one. This is the truth that many people miss. Many rich people have everything and don't value how rich they really are. And those people come through like bulldozers, smashing and dashing everything in their path. But only in the small details does the true beauty lie. Just remember that and you will come much further in your life than you expected.

Love, family, and kindness are the pillars on which society stands. They are the most important things. Societies aren't built on concrete and money. Money is just a tool used by people to accomplish their goals. The man who says that he can buy anything with money never actually had any. You can't buy health for money, only medicine. You can't buy love with money, only sex. You can't buy rest for money, only a bed. You have to understand that real love is free, the rest is priceless and the heart is only at peace when you love yourself for who you are. You are loved, you are important, you are perfect for just being who you are. The most important thing is that you shouldn't hurt others. Evil comes back with evil and good comes back as good. You can't just go around breaking everything and hating everyone for who they are. If you want to change the world, first you must look inside yourself. Because most of the time, you hate the world for treating you wrong, but you have to be open to the idea that you are the one who is wrong. Sometimes just one mistake can ruin your entire life, but life goes on. You forget your flaws, you leave the past behind and go to the new future that is ahead of you. That's how life goes. People can't just exist for their wishes and desires, you have to have more values in life than just satisfying your basic needs. If we were all like that, then we would be nothing more than animals. Sometimes the smallest act of kindness and dedication becomes like the ripple that goes through water and sparks thousands of hearts. Dedication to one another is the biggest gift that anyone can give. We have to remember that the only goal in life is to help one another. The ones who seek power and wealth usually end up broken. The real values are in small acts of kindness given by people, day by day. If you dedicate your life to caring for someone else, you will be the most gifted person than anyone could be. Caring for your loved one or caring for the person who is important to you is the greatest gift that anyone could give. You don't have to be wealthy to be rich. Some people are so poor in the heart that they seek only those funny papers or the numbers in the bank account. To have money is not a sin, but to live only for the money and build your life only around money is how you build a road to disaster. If you choose wealth you have to choose life. And nothing is more important than life.

I cared for that Asian girl who was assigned to me; helped her to look after the crops, to take care of the food. I taught her to hide the best food for herself and for her family. Many times I prayed to God for her to be happy one day, with a decent and honorable man. I cared for her like a child, because she was like a child and sometimes I thought that I would do the most horrible thing to anyone who would hurt her and no money in the world would save this person. I couldn't understand how anyone could do such horrible things to that sweet Polish girl we all so respected.

NEW CHAPTER

One day something really important happened. Joseph Stalin died in 1953 and we knew that every political prisoner was free to go home. I knew what I had to do. I packed my bags, took a small package with bread and milk and started my journey. I didn't have a map or anything that could guide me, but I had a few companions and the doctor gave me a compass. A few other Lithuanian people from the village were keeping me company. We decided to keep a secret of who we were and what our destination was and started our journey. We went on side roads and asked the directions for the local people. Almost all of them were friendly and helpful. Many of those people remember the horrors of war and we used to sit and chat about their stories with them. We heard many tragic stories and painful destinies. So many people were touched by the war and we thought that our destiny was hard. Many people were in physical and emotional pain and were struggling; many had lost someone from the hands of Nazis or their own people. Many were imprisoned falsely and accused of the crimes they didn't do. Many had scars from the war they could never forget. Russia was full of suffering and pain, but from that pain, there was new life beginning to grow. We saw young children running in the streets, playing games and just fooling around. They were happy, the war had ended and the new generation seemed hopeful about the future. Russian people seemed to amaze me every time I met them; with such pain in their eyes, they always sought for hope. They were always stronger than we could ever imagine. The strength in their spirit was immeasurable. People who lost everything in their life could see happiness in simple things of life; that was a real miracle. Their hope for a new life was growing slowly, there were new buildings build, new cities springing up, people were singing and dancing in the streets. A new hope was just around the corner and we all enjoyed it. When we traveled through Russia, we saw so many warm-hearted people almost everyone invited us with a smile. We tried to avoid the big city centers so we traveled through the villages and the smaller cities. People were smiling and they often gave us some food for the road. This journey was the best we had experienced in our lifetime. We tried to avoid people in uniforms, especially KGB or NKVD officers. They could ask us for documents and we would have none. We tried to stay as low profile as possible because we didn't know what would happen to us if we were caught without any documents. But we knew we had to return home. Our home was the only destination we could choose because we all wanted to return to our country. Those open fields they were so mesmerizing. After all, Lithuania was our home our only best hope for the future. The more we traveled, the more we expanded our knowledge. The horrible truths of the war were narrated by the people. How the Nazis burned the whole villages with people in them and other atrocities. Those stories were very terrible. Sometimes I wished I hadn't heard them. Many people suffered from the war and the horrible destiny they faced was terrible.

I traveled through roads and small villages. The journey was hard and sometimes I would almost lose myself, but I carried on. I wanted to return home to Lithuania, that was my ultimate destination. I just wanted to return home.

Everyone wants to be special and unique, but we are special in our own way. No one could be like you and no one can take your place. You are unique and so special and so important, you can't even imagine. If someone harmed you, he has harmed the whole universe, because you are your own universe, your own world. You have a set of skills that no one possesses; there can be no other John or Mary or Sam or Ashanti or Mombeko or Selena or Mei or Li Yong or Abigail or you. The world is special and has all the colors of a rainbow. If everyone were the same the world would probably be boring. Oh wait; we tried that already, it was called communism. Everybody has their own space in the world and that place is especially for you. You have your spot, your voice, your tone, your thought, your idea, your dream, your reality, your love, your chance, and nobody can take it away from you, because it is yours. Your dream is waiting there, secretly hidden from everybody else and kept there only for you and you only. So relax, breath in, sit on the rooftop and shout "the world is mine!"

My journey through Russia wasn't easy, so don't expect that your journey will be easy too. After all the magic happens when you push harder and harder. You have to press on even if the KGB police are chasing you or you have nothing to eat that day, or your life is a mess. Collect the broken piece of yourself and push on forward. That's how heroes are made. Heroes are the ones who go the extra mile and the ones who try when everything fails. Sometimes your life will be hard, sometimes even super hard, but you mustn't forget your goal and push on. After all, you are the master of your universe and you are the writer of your book.

When we all traveled through villages, people asked us many questions. Who were we? Where we were traveling? We explained that we were returning home from the lumber factory, so we were practically telling the truth. Many women wanted us to stay because strong and healthy men were scarce after the war. Women wanted families, but many men died in the war or were crippled by the bullets or bombs. Life wasn't easy for the Russian people; many of them had horrible memories from the time of war. Those memories haunted them all of their life. I had the same problem. I used to wake up at night from the horrors I had seen in the gulag. The people didn't mind me scaring them at night, because many of them had faced similar horrors. None should ever forget the horrors of the Second World War, because the lessons we learned in the war were the most important lessons in the 20th century.

We traveled through forests full of hungry wolfs, we waddled through the lakes and swamps, and we made soup from mushrooms and ate forest berries. The road was full of obstacles and challenges.

We never knew we could learn so much and so fast; we helped other villages with their simple problems and they welcomed us with open hands. Our farming and cattle experience was always welcomed by the locals and they couldn't understand how we knew so many things. Our help and support were always greeted with smiles and generosity. A loaf of bread and vegetables was the currency we needed to continue our journey. And we marched on forward. Some villages had only women and children in them because men were working in the factories or were heavily wounded. It was hard to go through such villages because you could see the women's eyes looking at you with the hope of a family. But you had to make a hard choice to leave and continue the journey home. We all had one destination; our homeland. That was the most important destination for all of us. In one village, we were very welcomed; the people were joyful and happy to see us. They welcomed us with open arms. We helped as much we could and they prepared a big table for us. The village had lots of women, children, and a few older people. We got along with the older people pretty well, they told us their stories and we told some of ours. This village was special; it had one of the nicest people we have seen. There was a woman in that village, she was really beautiful and she stood out from the rest, because of her bright smile and a warm heart. She was sweet and kind. It was easy to fall in love with her. She looked after one of us with some extra care and attention. After a few days, one of us settled in that village, because of that beautiful and warm-hearted woman. After all, love is love and nothing is more important than finding a place where you belong. That man was lucky, the woman was sweet and caring, and I'm sure they made a good couple.

We carried on with our journey. The people of the village gave us directions to follow a river and continue on until the nearest village where we could find help and support. They said the road would be long, but less dangerous following another road that lead to a small city that had a police station with a really bad reputation. We agreed with the villagers and followed the river. The road was hard because of the high grass and other unpleasant plant life. We got some skin burns from some plants and some rashes too.

However, the most important thing was that we found some villagers in the field who gave us some food and drink. Most villagers were nice and gave us something for the road and we continued on. They told us stories about the criminal mass murders of Jews performed by the Nazis and survivors of the holocaust told the horrible stories about how German soldiers killed old people, women, and even children and buried them in mass graves. No one was spared, but a few people lived on to tell the story. They were hungry and weak, but they still managed to survive through these horrors. The Nazi soldiers spared no one; the Jewish population was being exterminated without any remorse or concern. They weren't even considered people; they were seen as a disease that had to be eliminated. The Second World War was truly a horror for anyone who had a Star of David on his chest. The ones who survived told unbelievable stories of courage. The people, who survived the holocaust have the most interesting stories that anyone could tell you. They are bright people with shining hearts and full of wisdom. Those people have lived through horrible Nazi oppression and dehumanization. They are the true heroes who tell a story of the horrible Nazi holocaust machine and their voice will be heard through the decades to come.

Sometimes, I thought that those things weren't possible, but those stories were true. People tortured people and committed crimes against humanity in such large proportions that it is impossible to comprehend. How could people be so naïve? How could they follow the orders of such a madman like Hitler? Why did so many people follow a leader so blindly that they didn't even understand what they were doing? How could they have been so easily brainwashed by one man, whose only desire was power? These are the questions that must be answered by our future generations because the mistakes of the past can't be repeated. We have to stand our ground and ensure that this will never happen again and we will never bend or break for anyone except our families and loved ones.

Our journey continued. Sometimes, we were greeted like royalties and sometimes people would spit on us. Russia was a real mystery to me. This country had so many colors and so many different people; you couldn't distinguish one person from another. All the villages were different from the other, some had peace and harmony and others were like pots of fire burning in anger at each other. Sometimes I wondered why there is such diversity in every small village. Probably it was because people in the villages helped one another and in other villages, people just wanted to use each other and spread anger among people. The true hell and heaven are really inside of us and only we choose which side to pick. Our inner self-growth must be the main concern for anyone who walks on this earth. If we could control our thoughts, our minds, and our inner selves, we would have control of our life. We tried to avoid the villages with lots of drunks on the streets, because drunken people couldn't handle themselves and quickly could get in a fight or some other trouble. We also evaded villages with lots of loose women too. They always tried to pick our pockets and asked too many questions and we had to be discreet about our destination and about our past.

Something was still was haunting us. What we will do when we will get to Lithuania. How we will get work? What will the KGB do with us if we would get caught? Those questions were essential to us because our past was eating away at us. We had to keep as low as possible because we didn't know what we could run into and what trouble awaited us in the future. We escaped the gulag, but could we escape our past and live like normal people again? Those experiences bothered us to the core. We were exiles and had lost all connections to Lithuania. What will become of us, would we be sent back or interrogated? Will we be able to return like nothing happened? How will our future change? These were the questions we worried about the most because Lithuania was still under control of the Soviet Union; that meant that the people of the KGB were still in power in our country and they still had a strong grip on all sorts of decisions. Many people feared the KGB because it was a powerful organization that controlled many aspects of people's lives in the Soviet Union.

The KGB was the most secretive, most informed, most advanced and most powerful organization in the Soviet Union. Everybody feared them. They had total control over people's life and any swing in the wrong direction could quickly get you in trouble, in prison or something worse. People in the KGB were on top of the game in espionage and counterintelligence; they had all the keys to all the doors, they knew everything and anything that was needed to carry on their work. They had their spies in all the countries and they were prepared for anything. The only thing that crippled them was the fall of the Soviet Union. We all knew that one day we would have to face the people from the KGB and we were certain it wouldn't be a pleasant conversation, but we had to carry on; we had to march forward to our destination.

Important things are the ones that we ignore most of the time. These things include the care of our parents, the love of a pet, or a smile from a stranger. Many things are hidden from us because we don't bother to look. Nature holds the most secrets we usually don't see. Small details that inspire us and make us wonder how we didn't see it earlier. Every creature on this planet has beauty. You can see the beauty of nature everywhere like ducks, swans, storks, other small birds. They make us feel at ease; the beauty of nature is making our time valuable. When we are on a journey, we are so into ourselves and the small problems that we don't bother to look around and to spot the beauty of nature. Sometimes we could see roaders walking by or a small rabbit or fox running through the woods. Everything in nature is beautiful, you just have to relax and see it. The secrets are hidden from us because we don't bother to stop and look at the things that are most important. After all, we are all connected with the chain of life. Nature is like a tree of life that connects everything and if we destroy the branches of that tree of life, we risk swinging the balance of life to a very dangerous position. The tree of life protects us and gives us everything we need to survive. If we put the tree of life in danger and we use nature's resources disrespectfully, we risk veering into a very risky road that has only darkness and pain at the end of it.

We decided to take a break from our journey. There was a small village that looked pretty decent and the people seemed nice and helpful. We stayed there for a night to recover our strength. The people were friendly and the women seemed caring. So we thought we could rest a little, and in the meantime, help the villagers. We explained to them how to properly plant potatoes, we told them about fertilizer from cows and pigs, we taught them how to hide their harvest from unwanted guests, we explained about values and helped them around their farms. We tried to help them however we could. They welcomed us with open hands and they were really good people. The women told us their stories and their tragedies, elderly people listened to our advice, children wanted to cheer us up. It was a wonderful place somewhere on the outskirts of nowhere. It made us calm down a little. We planned to stay there for a few days to regain our strength and recover our food supply. The women were amazed that we all were against alcohol because many men in the village would have a drink or two. Many people considered us very intelligent and wise; they had no idea where we came from.

Some women stared at us like we would be their next husbands. We tried not to reveal much about ourselves because we still thought we could still be in trouble. People were sincere. They helped us heal some of our wounds on our feet from the long journey. They had good knowledge of herbs and medicine. They put something around our feet and the pains quickly wore off.

They were really nice people. We struck gold and wanted to stay longer to recover from our travel. The women were sweet and caring they helped us by giving us fresh milk and sweet cheese. We felt like kings or royalty in that town. Some of our men even thought about settling in that village. The women were really sweet, caring and beautiful. They helped us anyway they could. The men didn't like us much, but somehow, we got along with them too. They were smart people, so we didn't have lots of problems explaining to them that we weren't a threat and that we mean no harm not to them nor their daughters or women. We laughed and told funny stories we heard from other villagers. We danced with the grannies of that small village and we made corollas for the women. The people were impressed by the skills and knowledge we passed on to them. They learned many things about agriculture from us. We were like open books of knowledge that passed on our skill set to them. It was one of the most pleasant visits we had yet and we wanted it to last. We had really connected with the people and they really were open to welcome us among them. Even elderly people liked us. Somehow, this small village was the most beautiful village, from both the outside and the inside, we ever encountered. We placed our hopes and dreams in that village because the people were kind and generous.

One of us had a crush on a very beautiful young girl. They were meeting each other more and more and it seemed it was a love of huge proportions. The girl was sweet and elegant. She was so beautiful that even the sun would be jealous. The girl was also intelligent; she saw our way of life and accepted us pretty quickly. We were all astounded by her looks and knowledge. We were really excited that one of us caught her eye. They were meeting almost every day and talked for hours and hours. They were a sweet couple and all of us wanted them to make it.

But, as usual, bad eyes quickly caught them up. One person in that village was different. A young eighteen-year-old boy liked the girl too. He was in love with her too and he decided to inform the authorities about us. He picked up his stuff and decided to go to the nearest town and rat on us. One smart old lady quickly understood what he was planning and quickly told us about the boy's plan. We had no choice because soon the KGB would be in that village. We took what we could, the villagers gave us as many supplies we needed, the lovers kissed for the last time and we were off to our new destination. The villagers told us about a small river we needed to follow and we quickly reached that river. KGB officers could have dogs, so we couldn't risk it; we decided to go through the river as far as we could. Our feet were heavy from the long walk through the river. We were all wet and tired from walking down the river, but our spirits were strong; we knew we had our destination to reach and the destination was home. We all wanted to get back to Lithuania. All of us were strong and determined men, we had our spirits tested in the gulag and we didn't fear anyone. We tried our chances at some other villages, but most of them were small with lots of broken and sad people. We helped them how as best as we could, but most of those people were selfish and not determined to work hard. It was clear we had to march on to our destination, leaving those poor villages behind. The closer we got to Lithuania, the more desperate we were to reach our goal. It was clear that our destination was the most important thing to us and nothing else really mattered. We used a compass we acquired from the doctor at the gulag. So, we had no problem navigating through the hard roads and terrains. The compass was a real lifesaver, it helped us numerous times. We had lots of supplies, so we tried to avoid villages for a while. We hid in the forests and tried to travel as far as possible. We would walk many kilometers and avoid roads and train tracks. Our food supply was slowly depleting, but we tried to eat as little as possible because the KGB could be waiting for us in the nearest village. Sometimes, we were paranoid, but in our position, there was no other choice. We could be hunted like animals; KGB probably used dogs so from time to time, we would walk through the rivers we came across. We were sure that soon we would be captured and sent back to Siberia or executed, but we gathered our strength and marched on. Our mission was clear; we had to reach Lithuania, no matter what. We were scared and desperate, but the next day we stood up and soldiered on. The whole Soviet system was against us, but it didn't matter, because we had our goal and purpose. Nothing, except himself, can break a determined man.

We were secretly visiting some villages to get supplies, but we kept our profile as low as possible. We got just what we needed and disappeared instantly. We always tried to be as unsuspicious as possible. We talked only when needed and only if necessary. One of us would infiltrate and get the supplies while others hid somewhere near the village. One unknown man was less suspicious than a bunch of unknown men. We tried our best to be invisible and we succeeded. There was a big forest ahead of us and we dove into that forest, followed a river and went deeper and deeper into that forest. We knew that our destination was somewhere on the other side of that forest. We had supplies, but we didn't know how big the forest was.

Somehow, we found an old cabin. It was a forester's cabin. The man who was living in that cabin wasn't very friendly at first. He came outside with a gun and asked us what we were searching for in a forest. He asked us many questions and after some time he lowered his gun and invited us in. He was living with his daughter and his daughter was a real beauty; one of us couldn't keep his eyes off her. The forester knew we needed directions, so he wanted to make a deal with us. He would offer us a map with the locations we needed if we would help him build a new home for him and his daughter. We agreed. We started to cut suitable trees for the forester's new home. First, we built a foundation for the home. We used all the materials we could get our hands on. Then we cut the trees and, one by one, we started to build the walls for the house. The forester was amazed that we were really good at building homes like that and he was even more impressed that we wouldn't drink at all. We had a sip, just to show respect to the forester and that's all. One of us was really interested in the forester's daughter; they would talk and spend time together. We tried our best when building a new home for the forester because we really needed a map and directions to our destination. It was very important to understand where we were and to know what road or river to follow next. The forester was a really friendly man and we told him a little about us. He understood us really quickly and gave us more food; he was also falsely imprisoned so he knew what trouble we were in.

We were all sweating so much like we never did before. The work was really tough, but our forester friend was always giving us a helping hand and good advice. We worked hard and tried our best because we really needed that map. That map was the key to our success and we would have done everything to get it. The forester's daughter and one of our companions were really into each other. We knew that we had to leave him here eventually because love was burning in his eyes. We did our job as best we could, used the techniques we learned in Siberia and that house will stand tall for many years to come. Finally, when we made doors and windows, the forester took out his map. He showed us where we were and that we still had a long road ahead of us. We looked at the map with excitement and found out that our compass was leading us in the right direction. We asked many questions about which road to take and the forester always gave us answers. When we finally finished the forester's new home, we were off to Lithuania. We left one love bird with the forester's daughter and continued on.

The road was still long, but we made an enormous leap forward. We could see bigger towns on the map and were able to avoid them. Every big town was a danger because of the KGB and we certainly didn't want to wake the lion to come after us. We used small rivers and lakes to hide our footprints. The most important roads and railroads also had to be avoided. We used our skills to get supplies from the small towns we ran into and we always kept a low profile. To be as discreet was our main concern; we knew what awaited us if we got spotted by the secret Soviet police. The KGB was the organization that should be feared the most as it had all the bad reputation possible. After all, they were the best at what they did in Russia and we had no documents. We took a chance and used a map to our advantage, it was like a gift from God because that map had all the destinations we had to avoid. We walked through the woods and hid in various places. We filled our supplies only when necessary and only when needed. We ate mushrooms, berries, and other forest goodies. We tried our best to avoid people and go to villages only when necessary and then we would disappear real quickly. We tried our best to be patient and, little by little, we were closer to our goal.

The woods were almost empty and we only saw a few animals like wolves and reindeers. Perhaps the animals avoided us or we tried our best not to run into anybody. The road was hard and our feet hurt from extensive walking, but we had our purpose and even sore feet couldn't stop us. Sometimes we ran into people looking for mushrooms in the woods, but we avoided them in order not to get spotted. We tried to avoid making a fire because we could be caught by anyone. The map was a huge help; we knew exactly where we could have problems and where there was less danger for us. Sometimes, we would enter small villages, with a lot of caution because every village could have KGB police or people who would ask too many questions. We almost adapted to forest life and entered a village only when supplies were needed. We got really good at spotting and understanding different people. We tried to talk as little as possible and kept a low profile. The road was hard, but we marched on; our goal was getting nearer and nearer, so we continued on.

One night, we had a very dangerous encounter. A few wolves surrounded us from all sides. There were 3 of them and they seemed very hungry and bared their teeth at us. They seemed really dangerous, coming at us from different sides. One of us took an ax and took a big blow at one of the wolves' head. The blow was fatal and the wolf dropped to the ground. After the defeat, the other wolves just ran away. It was a very dangerous encounter and we all felt lucky to survive it. Our journey continued on. The woods were filled with wolves so we tried to take roads through the open fields.

After a few days of walking and feeling tired as hell, we ran into an old farmhouse. The house seemed empty, but we found an elderly woman living in it. The woman was exceptionally bright and wise. She asked us to do a few chores and promised to give us supplies. We helped her with cows, pigs, and chickens. She seemed happy to find such good company and invited us to stay longer. We were really tired, so we had no other choice but to agree. She was a wonderfully bright woman, and eventually, we had no choice but to stay with her longer and learn something from her. She introduced us to Lev Tolstoy and Feodor Dostoevsky. She had literature like War and Peace, Anna Karenina and Crime and Punishment. We were very glad to have met such a wonderful old lady. We helped her around the farm as much as we could. She understood that we weren't locals and asked a few questions. She figured us out very quickly, so we had no other choice just to tell the truth. This lady asked us about the horrible conditions we had to face and then she cried. She asked if she could help us. We wanted to stay with her longer to recover our strength and she agreed to keep us longer. She was impressed that we weren't interested in alcohol, which was something new to her. She gave us her good bed sheets and we were very welcome at her small little house. She had problems walking, so we took care of her small farm as best as we could. We tried our best because she really welcomed us and understood our plight. There were people who were helping her too but they were from a village nearby and didn't come very often, so we were safe from unwelcomed guests.

She told us her stories about the war and that her only son died in the war. She was very upset when mentioning her son; she hated the war as much as we did. She told us that the war was very bad for many people and that it should never happen again. We all agreed because we all had suffered hard from the war and we all said that it should never happen again.

The old lady was very bright; her soul was like a crystal, and she loved every person she came across in her life. She said that some people come to our life as blessings and some people come to our lives as lessons. She was a really amazing person who taught us many things and we listened to her every word. She was also a religious person, praying every night. She told us about her life and how she got married. After some time, her husband died from some kind of disease and she was left alone with her son. Her son helped her around the farm; the work was hard but they managed to put food on the table. She told us about the war and the many people who died during the war. She cried when she remembered her son. He was a good person and he helped others.

She treated us like her children; she gave us good food, and to thank her, we did our best with her farm; we built one additional building for her cows and chickens and we could all see she was very pleased with us. We also cleaned the pig pit and build her a new toilet. We helped with the chickens, cows, pigs, and potatoes. We felt immense respect for that woman and we had to help her as best as we could. She was happy to see us work on her farm and wanted to thank us. We agreed that her advice and a good word were all that we needed. The loaves of bread she gave us were also very important. We wanted to leave, but she insisted that we stay a few more days. She was a very bright person; she told us many things about faith, ethics, values, hope, and farming. We were pretty literate in those fields, but she really helped us to broaden our views.

Every day went on like in a fairy tale, we helped her around the farm and she helped us with our broken souls. She was the brightest person we had ever encountered, she taught us not to seek revenge, but to seek happiness and fulfillment. She taught us to follow our dreams and continue what we started and, most importantly, have a good life. This person had such a bright heart and such a warm personality, that we all were amazed by how she could be that wise. We decided to keep her company longer. We fixed her fence and took care of her yard. We were determined to learn as much as possible from this woman. She taught us such things we could never imagine. She was like a bright spark in an uncertain world, whose wisdom and knowledge was endless. By learning so much from her, we gained a solid foundation on what we had planned for our future. We knew that the lessons we got there will be the most important lessons in our lives and the books she showed us opened many doors for our future. We were still feeding pigs, milking cows and gathering eggs, but we did it out of the highest respect for that person who made us understand the lessons of life. She always looked happy and her mind was clear. She was a warm person whose heart had no limits. We told her about our struggles and she cried listening to our stories. We were welcomed at her place and she told us that she had never met such bright people like us before. We tried to cheer her up and told her funny stories from our youth; we all laughed and enjoyed our time.

We tried to fix her farming equipment like buckets and other items. She was pleased that we were helping her and made us fresh potato soup. We gathered around the fireplace later at night and gazing into the stars. We felt like normal people again; we were having fun, eating freshly baked potatoes and drank warm milk. We listened to our elderly lady and her life stories. Her story was like a book filled with bright and dark chapters. We all knew she was a special person and that we could count on her and she will never betray us. We forgot the pain, the hunger, and the horrors we had had to face. Everything was different and we felt human again. She had something that mesmerized us; the light inside of her was like a shining beacon. We agreed to stay a little longer. We helped her out as much as we could; we tried our best to fix her small house and her barn. We cut grass for her cows and took it to the barn; we helped her around the house and fed the chickens. We wanted to help her as much as possible because nothing else was more important than compassion; we wished we could do more for her.

We knew there would be a day when we would be parted and had to move on in our journey. We wished that day would never come. That woman was the most wonderful person we encountered; we wished we could stay with her longer. She understood we had to leave because nothing was more important than our home. We cried when we left her home because she was the brightest and sweetest person we have ever met. With tears in our eyes, we left her and continued our journey to our home. She taught us so many things that we could never forget her for. She was the brightest spark in our lives, but we had to leave for home.

Our journey home was long; we traveled through forests, swamps, lakes and empty fields. Our feet were tired and our bodies were getting weaker, but we continued our journey. Our destination was the most important thing to us and using a map and a compass helped us to reach our destination. We parted ways, said our goodbyes to each other, but we all agreed to meet from time to time and share the knowledge and wisdom we acquired on our long journey. We agreed to help others in need and help the people who were most desperate. When we got back home we had to learn the hard truth and understand that our destiny was much harder than we have imagined.

NEW CHAPTER

When I was getting closer to my home my heart was filled up with joy and happiness, I thought that this destination would lead me back to my home and my parents. I felt like my heart would explode as I was getting closer and closer to my homeland. I saw a young boy who was taking care of a cow near a lake where I lived and asked him where my family lived. The boy burst in tears and told me that he was my brother and my mother and father were dead and that he was one of two brothers who survived. We gathered inside our old home and cried the whole night. I told them what I had learned and what I endured. My brothers were living in poverty and hardship. When I came along, things were starting to get better. I taught the locals the secrets of survival and how to outthink and prevent the Soviet troops from taking away all of the food, how to help others, sharing and surviving the hardest of times. We got used to hiding food and teaching others how to do it. Somehow, my knowledge became crucial for our survival. We worked day and night in the fields and tried our best to help other people and share my knowledge.

Next came the collectivization of farms; all the animals and land were taken away from the people, people were sent to work in the collective farms where, for their hard work, they were given only scraps of food and all the food was sent to bigger cities where there was work in bigger factories. The people left their farms and went to the cities. I too traveled to the city, taking my brothers with me. We worked in the fertilizer plant and we tried our best to fit in. Work was hard, but we had to put the bread on the table. The more I worked, the easier it seemed. We weren't rich; quite the opposite, we were very poor people. The pay was low and the hardships we had to endure were horrible, but it put food on the table. My brothers started to drink and that was something I hadn't expected. I tried to teach them that drinking was bad and they shouldn't do that; drinking made them weaker and it was a way through which the government controlled them. Soviets used alcohol to control masses of people and alcohol was the main problem in the Soviet Union. Almost everybody was drinking too much. I was devastated because I knew what alcohol could do to a man.

Somehow, the KGB found out that I was in Siberia and ordered me to report to the local office. There were two harsh people sitting in the room and sizing me up from top to bottom. I was nervous and a little scared, but the times were different and their tone was softer; they didn't beat me, just asked a bunch of questions and wanted me to feel uncomfortable. I felt they wanted to scare me into not telling anybody about the horrible things I went through in Siberia. After that meeting, I was devastated, but life always has two sides.

A woman introduced me to her sister. She was really sweet and beautiful and I have never met someone like her. Her heart was pure and her smile was magical. Every time we kissed, I felt a shiver go through my body. Love is blind and she didn't even notice my bald head. I couldn't let go of such a wonderful woman and soon after, we got married. Our life was full of happy moments together. Every touch of her skin made my heart pound faster and faster.

One day, she felt different. After seeing a doctor, we found out that she was pregnant. We put every dream and hope into that child and we wanted him or her to have a better life than we did. We wanted him/her to be happy and to be loved and cared for. We prepared everything for our new child. We did all the Herculean work; we got the bed, and we collected sheets for diapers.

The belly was growing bigger. We felt happy. When the time of birth finally came, my daughter was born dead. We cried all the time and just wanted our pain to end. We held and supported each other the best we could because nothing was more important than our child. We prayed to God to give us hope. We didn't know what we did wrong to deserve this, we hadn't hurt anyone and we had both suffered so much and had come through such a hard life. We just hugged and cried, the feelings were horrible; it felt like the ground broke beneath our feet. Nothing can be worse than losing your child. Nothing is more painful to a woman than to lose something that you carried, cherished and waited for your whole life. When this happens, a man must support his woman, no matter what and at this moment a woman is very vulnerable and only a truly strong man can support the love of his life; only cowards and weak men leave the woman in such a condition when she is most vulnerable. I wasn't a coward. I took the dead baby and buried it in the local cemetery near the hospital where she gave birth. From time to time, we visited the cemetery and prayed for her. We were devastated, for 6 months she cried and only hugs and kisses helped her through such horrible times.

One day I got a letter from the doctor who saved me in Siberia. He wanted to move to Lithuania. I agreed and tried to help him as much as I could. There were people who I knew who worked in a hospital and they helped him get a job.

I told him about my loss. He calmed me down and told that this happens very often with a first child and that the next child would probably be healthy. We met often and talked about our days in Siberia. He told me that many things had changed, people were more at ease, the government didn't press people so hard and everything was changing for the better. I was glad to hear this. After all, I bonded with those people and cared for them. He told me that many people left the village to find work in bigger cities and he also wanted change so he decided to live in Lithuania. He remembered me and my stories about my beautiful country. So the doctor decided to travel here to Klaipeda. I was glad that he chose to travel here. I helped the doctor as much as I could with the connections I had. Many people from the gulags had underground connections within Lithuania and the underground movements of people who wanted to see a free Lithuanian country were spreading all over the country.

One day, we drove to the village to meet my wife's mother. She had lots of children and my wife was her youngest daughter. They both cried when she heard that we lost our baby. When we got married, I made a promise to help her mother with farm work. She didn't have lots of animals, many of them were taken to kolkhoz, but she had a cow, a few chickens, and a small beautiful farm. We stayed there as much as we could in order to help with farm work. Those days were hard; we had to help her but at the same time we had to return to Klaipeda and go to work in the factories. I had to work harder because my wife also worked hard in those days. There was no easy work for women, sometimes women worked as hard as men did. Socialism meant that everyone was equal and labor rights were equal too. Sometimes, women had to carry bricks and heavy items. Today, in modern Western society, hard labor is considered a man's work and women are given easier tasks. Of course, a woman can do every type of work and the socialist system proved that, making women work as much as men did. But a strong and intelligent man will never allow his woman to work too hard while he is lying on the sofa.

I worked hard; the dust from the fertilizer was getting inside my lungs. My work was never easy and those times there was no easy work. We didn't have office jobs back then, supermarkets didn't exist and the logistics companies were yet to be seen. But we had love, we had one another and that was all that mattered. We mourned for a year for our daughter. We couldn't do anything; we were so desperate. It was the hardest loss we had ever experienced and we hoped that the next time, we would make it.

Life always has a way. Sometimes we have to wait for something beautiful to happen, but it is all worth it. Love is blind, love is precious, she is kind, doesn't envy, doesn't feel anger, she comes through everything, she prevails and she never ends. If you think that you lost love or you will never love again, you are wrong. Sometimes love heals even a broken soul and true love will never leave you; it stays in your heart and your dreams forever. If your love is true she will stay with you forever and true love lives on even after you die. Sometimes love shows herself even in the person you least expected; he might not be that beautiful nor that smart, but he could love you more than life itself and follow you through your whole journey, leaving a special mark in your life and change you forever.

Once, I saw a girl in the church. She had burns on her, but I didn't notice her burns at all. She was beautiful despite her scars. Her light shined through her and I watched her like seeing someone landing from the skies. I saw her with a man and then I understood how happy that man was because to live with such a bright soul is a real blessing from God.

If everybody knew how much they had, they wouldn't chase something they didn't need. Sometimes I wonder why many people are so unhappy. They are unhappy not because they don't have a thing. They are unhappy because they want something that others have, but they don't know the price the other had to pay to get that. You don't need a Lamborghini to be happy; you need love and attention from your family. The good health of your family, the love of your children and the smile on your wife's face is all you need. No luxury item can give you happiness, no new technology can give you satisfaction and no material thing can give you fulfillment. If you put your energy into material things, your happiness will be temporary. However, if you put your energy into helping others and serving a greater cause, your happiness will be endless. Mother Theresa said: "I have found the paradox, that if you love until it hurts, there can be no more hurt, only more love." She also said: "It's not how much we give but how much love we put into giving."

Sometimes I dream of a better world with no wars, no more sickness, no more drugs, and alcohol. I dream of a world where all the children live in caring families. I dream that people will find peace in their souls and will live a good life without hurting each other. A life is a happy life only when lived in harmony with others and peace within yourselves.

For a year, my wife and I lived in sorrow; we thought about our child and how hard it was for us. But we carried on, we worked our best, we cried our tears. Most importantly, we lived. We helped our mother on the farm and the work at the farm united us more like nothing before. We became closer and closer. My wife's mother was very wise and we listened to her as much as we could. She was tough, but she loved us. She had a strong arm and kept us in place.

One sunny morning, we went to gather hay in the big fields. We worked hard and when we got tired, we lay on the big stack of hay. I looked into her eyes and kissed her slowly then I kissed her neck. Our bodies shivered together. The kisses went on and on; we just couldn't let go of each other. I looked into her eyes and smiled. She kissed me like there was no tomorrow. I slowly took her clothes off and touched every part of her body while kissing her beautiful lips. We were so much in love that nothing else really mattered. Our bodies were close to each other and we couldn't let go of one another. I took my clothes off. We kissed and couldn't stop touching each other. We couldn't let go. We danced the dance of love together.

When we returned home, our mother greeted us; she understood everything really quickly just by looking into our eyes. She gave us bread, made a bed for us, gave us a fresh cup of milk and sent us to sleep in a separate room. We were looking into each other's eyes like we hadn't seen each other before.

I slowly kissed her lips and she kissed mine, we sunk into each other's lips and didn't let go. We held each other in our arms and tried to be as quiet as possible. I kissed her neck and she shivered. I couldn't take my eyes off her; she was so beautiful. Her lips felt like cherries and feeling her warm body next to me was the most magnificent feeling I had ever felt. We lay naked and every touch of her sweet fingers was driving me mad. We were so much in love like never before, we couldn't keep our hands off each other. Our bodies were as one and our love was breathtaking. I told that I loved her and would never leave her. I told her that she was the most beautiful woman in the world and I would never hurt her and love her till the end of our days and I kept my promise.

After that day we knew we loved each other more and more and our love grew stronger. The more tears we cried, the more the hardships we endured, the stronger our love became.

My wife worked at a tree bark-peeling factory. The work was hard, now only done by men, but she endured. Work was hard as hell, but we had to survive, we needed the money. We also visited my wife's mother as much as we could, because there is nothing more important than family. Our love grew stronger and stronger; we had almost forgotten how we lost our child. We used to spend time in the shed full of hay, lying almost naked and all alone. I used to run my fingers on her wonderful legs and her whole body while kissing her softly like there was no tomorrow. The kisses were soft and gentle; I could never forget her smile when she looked at me with those sweet and gentle eyes. Her smile made me the happiest man on earth; she was like the flower that bloomed inside my hands. We were so much in love; her love for me inspired me to never give up no matter what, I was going to do everything in my power to make her happy. She was the brightest star in my universe.

After some time, we learned that my wife was pregnant again. We felt so much joy and happiness like never before. We were full of anxiety and we tried our best to protect the baby. Factory administration gave her easier tasks; taking care of the towels and gave her other easier work. We were happy to finally get a second chance to have our baby; this was like a blessing from God and we had waited for this child for our entire life. My wife's belly got bigger and my love for her got stronger. Nothing in my life was more important than her. I wanted the best for my child, I didn't want her to work as hard as we did and we wanted her to be healthy and happy. I was scared about her birth, but when our baby was born the smile on her face filled our hearts with happiness. She was so sweet, beautiful and lovely, that we couldn't keep our eyes off her. We changed her diapers many times and surrounded her with love. Every step of the way, we were there to protect her. Her lovely character and a beautiful soul were seen from the early days. She was full of energy and couldn't stay in one place. Sometimes, she would run away from us and we had to look for her. She was a good child; she always listened to us and helped us as much she could. She loved the animals on the farm and always looked at the bright side of life. Her love for life was amazing. Once, I saw her running through the fields and I remembered that she was that girl in my dreams who I saw when I was living in the Siberian village. I was so happy when I saw her and couldn't take my eyes off her. My eyes were full of tears and I knew that this was the biggest gift from God I could ever receive.

"Daddy, why are you crying? Is there something wrong?" She asked.

"No, I'm just happy. Those are the tears of joy," I replied.

"I didn't know that. I only cry when I fall down or hurt myself."

She used to climb the sweet cherry trees at our relatives' village and eat as much she could. She looked like a monkey when climbing those giant trees. We were a bit scared but she wouldn't climb down. Those cherries were her weak spot. When my wife and I would lay in the bed, our daughter would give one hand to me and the other to my wife and we would lay like this for some time, feeling each other's hands and that amazing connection we had. We were full of joy and happiness because our daughter seemed like the most wonderful gift from God we could ever receive. She was a very good child in school and played the accordion and also started playing basketball. We didn't know where she got so much energy and passion for life. She liked to dance a lot and we had to take her home from her dances from time to time. She was also very energetic and boys were all around her. She liked to tease them, but never gave them any bad ideas. She was a real coquette with boys and enjoyed their attention.

Once, she took a relative's motorcycle and tried to ride it as fast she could. She crashed the motorcycle into a ditch, but gladly, everything was fine and she didn't break anything. She was a wild one, but she always had a good heart and saw the best in others. She loved kids and when she enrolled in the university, she chose pedagogy. While at the university, she fell in love and married. In those days, the church was considered removed from the government, because of the Soviet ideology, so she married her husband in the church, in secret. The church was small, somewhere in the outskirts of the countryside, but the ceremony was beautiful. The priest performed the illegal ceremony in secret, but we were all happy and joyful that our daughter was married in church and gave wows in front of God.

After a few years, she had a son. That was the second most joyful thing after my daughter's birth. He was so good and wonderful that I could never imagine feeling so much happiness in my life. We were the happiest people in the world; we had everything.

We lived in a single-flat apartment, meant for our family and my daughter with her husband. We also had a small garden with trees that produced all sorts of fruits like apples, pears, plums, cherries; we also had carrots and potatoes. I remember our wonderful time in the greenhouse where we had tomatoes. The beauty of life is simple. You have to cherish what you have and live a simple life, every small moment of life counts, every breath of air, every smile from your neighbor, your friend or somebody you don't know. I knew I did love my life and I lived my life to the fullest as much as I knew how and as much I could.

Like every story, this story has to come to an end. My clock stopped in 1986. You probably know this date; it's the same year when the Chernobyl nuclear power plant exploded, releasing tons of toxic particles into the atmosphere. The Soviet gulags didn't kill me, but the pride and carelessness of the Soviet scientists did. I had problems with my prostate earlier, but the toxic radiation from the Soviet nuclear plant sealed my fate. I died in an operation room in Klaipeda. The doctors couldn't do anything. But my last wish in the Soviet gulags came true; I died in my country and lived a wonderful life. When I was chopping trees in the Soviet gulag, I never knew that I would have a family and that my family would be so amazing.

But this isn't the end of my story.

Very soon the Soviet system started to crack. The Chernobyl incident crippled the government, the war in Afghanistan was lost, the price of oil dropped to record lows, former Soviet territories were seeking independence. The giant and mighty Soviet Union was falling apart. On 23 August 1989 three Baltic States – Estonia, Latvia, and Lithuania formed The Baltic Way or Baltic Chain. It was a peaceful demonstration when approximately two million people joined their hands to form a human chain spanning 675.5 kilometers (419.7 mi) across the three countries. This was the first demonstration of such magnitude, comprising the people of three Baltic States who joined their hands for peace and unity. Lithuania declared its independence on March 11, 1990, and on January 13, 1991, Russian tanks rolled in the streets of Vilnius. People stood unarmed before the tanks and protected the TV tower and the parliament of the independent Lithuanian Republic. People sang songs and stood while soldiers hit them with the rifle handles. Not a single shot was fired at the Russian soldiers, but 14 Lithuanians died that day protecting their independent country. One woman, Loreta Asanavičiūtė, was rushed to the hospital because she was crushed by the tank. She asked the doctor if she could have children. The doctor just cried because he knew that she had only minutes to live.

On 26 December 1991 Union of Soviet Socialist Republics (USSR) was voted out of existence. Mikhail Gorbachev resigned and all the authority and powers were given to the first Russian president, Boris Yeltsin.

1 May 2004 Lithuania joined the European Union and on 29 March 2004, Lithuania joined the North Atlantic Treaty Organization.

My name is Jonas Racevičius. I was born in 1922 in a small village in Lithuania, near the lake Lukstas and this is my story.

Conclusion

My name is Jonas Racevičius, I was born in Lithuania in 1922 and this was my real story. I have seen lots in my lifetime. I have seen pain, I have seen death. But I have never seen so much hope as I did in the eyes of the Russian people. They stood before the odds; they managed to endure and pick up the lost pieces in the rubble and put it all back together. They suffered the most from the war. They made the biggest sacrifices. They had the odds stacked against them, but they overcame their difficulties. Most importantly, they fought for their loved ones and for their children. In my entire life, in Siberia, I saw the best and worst in people. Some of them were evil, some of them were ruthless, but most of them were kind, gentle and generous. They helped the ones who were hurt, and the ones in need. They gave their lump of bread and they knew the value of life. The most important thing in life is to love one another and in the end, the goodness in people will prevail, I know that.

Synopsis

This is a true story about a man, who survived the Soviet gulags, went through hell on earth in Siberia and returned home after Stalin's death on March 5, 1953. The story tells of his life in the gulag, his journey home, the impossible struggle and the will to survive the most horrible conditions imaginable. It is a story of hope and the victory of one man against the whole system of oppression and dehumanization. It's a true story of the fate of millions of Lithuanian, Latvian, Estonian, Polish, Belarusian, Ukrainian and Russian people. The Soviet machine sent doctors, teachers, writers, professors and anyone else who opposed their regime to the outskirts of the Siberian forests and wilderness. It's a story about those people. It's also a story of victory as the oppressor was defeated and the Soviet Union collapsed on the 26 December 1991.